A
Goju Ryu
Guidebook:

The Kogen Kan Manual for Karate

By
Michael P. Cogan, MSE
Forward By
Franco Sanguinetti

Order this book online at www.trafford.com
or email orders@trafford.com

Most Trafford titles are also available at major online book retailers.

Print information available on the last page.

ISBN: 978-1-5539-5846-8 (sc)

Trafford rev. 06/26/2018

www.trafford.com

North America & international
toll-free: 1 888 232 4444 (USA & Canada)
fax: 812 355 4082

Table of Contents

A Goju Ryu Guidebook:
The Kogen Kan Manual for Karate

Table of Contents

Table of Contents

Table of Contents

Forward

Since the early days of *Te*, *To-De*, or the later name of *Karate*, the art has been traditionally communicated and passed on in verbal form. This transmission has been conducted from one generation to another mainly from instructor to student, which included, in many cases, transmission from father to son. What was very important is that those instructors took their time and had the dedication to make sure that the knowledge that they possessed would not die with them. It is important to realize that each instructor that takes on this task also adds to his or her own research and training by doing so.

Not all martial arts practitioners become instructors, nor do all martial art instructors have the desire, energy and unselfish motivation to pass on their knowledge. It has been said that from one hundred practitioners that start the traditional training of *Karate*, only one will become a Black Belt. From those few who are privileged and dedicated to reach that level, even fewer will remain active in the arts for the rest of their lives. So, when I see someone like Sensei Michael Cogan spending time transmitting knowledge in a more modern media, providing others with a book for them to possess, which includes knowledge he has received as well as knowledge he has developed through years of dedicated training, I have nothing less to do than commend his unselfish and humble commitment to the martial arts community.

The years that I have known Sensei Cogan through his training in *Karate* and *Kobudo* has allowed me to know him not only as a *budoka* (practitioner of the martial arts), but most importantly, as a person. It is an honor for me to write this forward for this, <u>*A Goju Ryu Guidebook*: *The Kogen Kan Manual for Karate*</u>.

I can only say, "Job well done Sensei Cogan!"

Franco Sanguinetti
Bushikan Budo Kyokai

Dedication and Acknowledgements

Dedication

This manual is dedicated to my students, whether in the public school or in the dojo. By teaching them I get an endorphin rush that is a real supercharge! Teaching also helps open doors in my own training. I hope I never lose sight of the fact that the teacher-student relationship is symbiotic.

Acknowledgments

I would like to thank (alphabetically) Sensei Carter, Sensei Dascenzo, Sensei Hamilton, Sensei Higaonna, Sensei Hollingsworth, Sensei Ingles, Sensei Lobue, Sensei O'Hara, Sensei Olfs, Sensei Pralgo, Shihan Roseberry, Sensei Sanguinetti, Sensei Schweizer, Sensei Shingu, Sensei Spirito, Sensei Terrell, Sensei Wilson and Sensei Wolcott. I am very proud to have been associated, throughout the years, with so many people who have such a high degree of knowledge and abilities.

I would also like to thank my loving wife Lisa. She provided a lot of moral, grammatical and nutritional (she is a wonderful cook) support for me while writing this guidebook. It is very easy for me to realize that I am a very lucky man.

I owe Dan Tappe a debt of gratitude for training with me during a transitional time in my life. He also helped dot my "*i*'s" and cross my "*t*'s"! Thanks Dan!

A special thanks goes to my father, John P. Cogan. After he finished his book, _A New Order of Man's History_ (Elton-Wolf Publishing, 2001), I was inspired to strive ahead and not give up on this project.

To everyone who have helped show me the "Way" of karate, this is a big group which include many not listed here, "Domo Arigato Gozaimasu."

Michael P. Cogan, MSE

Name	in Japanese
Michael	マイケル

Maikeru

光源

About the Guidebook

A Goju Ryu Guidebook: The Kogen Kan Manual for Karate gives the reader a tool to navigate the history, exercises, equipment, techniques, kata (forms) and kumite (sparring) of Okinawan Goju Ryu Karatedo. The purpose of this guidebook is to serve as a training aid in furthering the development of karate students and instructors from the Kogen Kan specifically and all karate students generally; however, if it helps only one person, then I will consider it a success.

Please keep in mind that much of this information is in notation form and may only make sense with proper instruction. This guidebook is only a tool to help in the retention of instruction and is not a substitute for it. Also, please keep in mind, that although others have assisted with this guidebook, all errors are my own.

This guidebook is formatted in such a way as to be the beginnings of a filing and retrieval system. As each student collects more information, they can organize it by adding it to the "notes" area of the respective sections. It is hoped that all students will research, collect and share material about karate. It is this type of systematic approach that brings science to the art.

It is also written so that a lesson plan can be developed quickly by choosing one or more activities from several sections. If more details are needed while teaching, they can quickly referenced in the rest of the manual. Each chapter is given a table of contents to further hasten referencing. It has a spiral coil binding so it will lay flat for easy viewing during training. Large font also helps in referencing the information from a distance.

Much of this guidebook is written in Japanese. This is done for two reasons: first, it is important to learn Japanese, as it will help standardize everyone's martial arts training; and secondly, this will help keep this information in the purview of the serious. It is a barrier, which will hopefully weed out some who may not use the martial arts for purposes which they were intended, namely the protection of self and others.

Thank you for reading this guidebook.

Michael P. Cogan, MSE

Chapter 1

The Kogen Kan

Chapter 1 Table of Contents

From the library of

Name _____

Address _____

_____

Phone _____

E-mail _____

The Kogen Kan Mission Statement

The Kogen Kan is a traditional school that strives to provide students with safe, professional, world-class instruction on the history, techniques and virtues of Okinawan Goju Ryu Karatedo and Matayoshi Kobudo. While developing a strong mind, body and indomitable spirit, students learn to be self-disciplined, respectful, kind and honest.

The Kogen Kan Name

Kogen (n) light source
Kan (n) hall

The Kogen Kan is my choice for a dojo name. Kogen (pronounced koh-gen) is a very close phonetic translation of my name, Cogan, into kanji. It means "light source" or "source of light." Kan translates as "hall." Together the name translates as "The Hall of the Source of Light." I was reluctant to use this name at first, because I was afraid that it might sound terribly egotistical. However, with the proper explanation, I am sure people will understand that this name is not as grandiose as it may appear at first blush.

The Explanation: The night sky is full of millions of stars. Each one is a source of light. When people need to chart a course for a journey, they may use many stars in a variety of combinations. As they progress on their journey, they may need to use different stars. Each star has a value unto itself.

The night sky can be thought of a karate-do. Each star can be thought of as a dojo. All Dojos are sources of light. This dojo is one source of light among many. Some dojos are brighter and some are dimmer but each has a value unto itself. It is my hope that this dojo can help some people as they navigate on their journey through life.

The Insignia

This insignia was designed by this writer as a visual representation of many elements of traditional Okinawan Goju Ryu Karatedo.

The kanji on the insignia (top to bottom respectively) is *Go* and *Ju*. These represent the name of our karate style, which is *Goju Ryu*. *Go* translates as "hard" and *Ju* translates as soft. *Ryu*, which is not on the insignia, can translate as "style" or "school."

Behind the kanji is the Ying~Yang symbol. This symbol represents opposites such as "inhalation and exhalation," "day and night," "up and down" and "hard and soft." The idea that the Ying~Yang symbol represents "hard and soft" is of unique importance because this interpretation is reflected in the name *Goju Ryu*. Also of note is that the kanji printed in black is on the white part of the symbol and the kanji printed in white is on the black part of the symbol. This is because they are taking the place of two dots in the interior of each side, which are the color of the opposite side. The opposite color contained within each side of the symbol represents that there is never anything that is completely Ying or completely Yang.

A ring of gold around the insignia represents the marriage of all things. It also represents the eternal light upon which everything in this world are but shadows.

The Author's Lineage

I began my karate training in the fall of 1981 at Washington State University under the guidance of Sensei Steven Olfs, his teacher Sensei Michael Dascenzo and his teacher Shihan John Roseberry. Shihan Roseberry studied under Sensei Toguchi who was a direct student of Sensei Chojun Miyagi. Shihan Roseberry is the founder of Sho Rei Shobu Kan. I received my ranks of ju kyu through ni kyu from Sho Rei Shobu Kan.

In 1987, I moved to Camarillo, California. Then in 1995, after a long period of personal training, I began training with the International Okinawan Goju Ryu Karate Federation (IOGKF) under the guidance of Sensei Mel Prolgo and his teacher Hanshi Morio Higaonna. Sensei Higaonna has studied under several direct students of Sensei Chojun Miyagi. In 1996, I received my rank of ik kyu and in 1997 of Shodan. Both were from the IOGKF. 1997 was the year I began my association with Sensei Franco Sanguinetti. I received the Bushikan Karate and Kobudo Kyokai Spirit Award at Sensei Sanguinetti's August 1997 gasshuku.

Also, in 1997, I began training with Sensei Steve Wilson. He introduced me to hojo undo, renzoku and ground fighting. Sensei Wilson's teacher is Sensei Stan O'Hara. Sensei O'Hara has studied Goju Kai with the Yamaguchi family and Okinawan Goju Ryu with Sensei Higaonna. Sensei O'Hara is the founder of the Okinawan Goju Ryu Kenkyu Kai (OGRKK). I received my rank of Nidan from the OGRKK in August of 2000.

In 2001, I chose to become independent. This was a difficult time, but to quote an urban legend, "In Chinese there is no word for disaster, only opportunity." It was time for me to move on and step up to more responsibility. This is when my dojo, The Kogen Kan, was born. It is a small garage dojo, but what it lacks in size it makes up for in enthusiasm. Humble beginnings will hopefully lead to great things.

The Instructors

Introduction

We are fortunate to have various instructors provide guidance to students throughout their training. Some information about three of them are listed here. The instructors are presented in the chronological order in which I was fortunate enough to be introduced to them. They are Shihan John Roseberry, Morio Higaonna Sensei and Franco Sanguinetti Sensei.

Shihan John Roseberry

Shihan John Roseberry may be seen in Lincoln, Nebraska, and sometimes at local seminars. I first met Shihan Roseberry in 1981 in Pullman, Washington. Later I met him again in 1997. He looked virtually the same. I asked him his secret and he said, "I've stopped worrying." Good advice with a great outcome. The following biography can be found at the Sho Rei Shobu Kan website: http://www.radiks.net/~srsbk//index.html . The picture in this biography is courtesy of Shihan Roseberry.

Shihan John Roseberry, chief instructor, has been training in judo and karate since 1955. He studied judo under Matsumoto-Sensei and karate under Toguchi-Sensei in Okinawa, the birthplace of karate. He has trained at the Kodokan in Japan, as well as in China and Korea. Roseberry-Shihan teaches Okinawan Goju Ryu Karate, Kodokan Judo and Aikido. He presently holds an 9th degree black belt in karate, 7th degree black belt in judo and 3rd degree black belt in Aikido. Roseberry -Shihan served as an alternate to the 1964 U.S. Olympic Judo Team, was All-Marine Corps Champion seven times, All-Service Champion three times and was the only American to capture the All-Okinawan Judo Championship. He has been teaching martial arts in Lincoln, Nebraska since 1969. His dedication comes from training and discovering the answers through practice. In his schools, students often hear that the answer is on the floor, and he lives this maxim. He currently has students who have been with him for over twenty years practicing on a regular basis. Through his reputation and word of mouth, he has built an organization that spans the world with 28 member dojo. He has never solicited membership; all of the member dojo have either been founded by students who have moved away from the headquarters in Lincoln and felt the need to continue to be trained by Roseberry-Shihan, or have been dojo who have heard of him, seen him work and have requested membership.

The Instructors

Sensei Morio Higaonna

Sensei Morio Higaonna will be seen locally at seminars. He spends much of his time in Japan. His contributions to the world of karate include five books and a library of video works. He has trained many talented black belts who carry on his legacy. The International Okinawan Goju Ryu Karate-Do Federation (IOGKF) web address is http://www.iogkf.com/ . He is a very strong and talented practitioner. It was an honor for me to test in front of him for my Shodan in 1997.

The author (right) with Higaonna Sensei

The picture in this biography was taken at the Suiho En Dojo in May, 2001 and is the property of the author.

Sensei Morio Higaonna, 9th Dan, is the Chief Instructor of the International Okinawan Goju Ryu Karate-Do Federation (IOGKF) and a member of the All Japan Budokan. He was born in 1938 in Naha, the capital city of Okinawa. His father, a police officer, evacuated the family to southern Japan prior to the American invasion of Okinawa in 1945. The family returned shortly after the war ended. Sensei Higaonna began his martial arts training by watching his father teach students Shoin Ryu. At the age of 16 he began training in Goju Ryu at the late founder's garden Dojo under the guidance of An'ichi Miyagi Sensei. An'ichi Miyagi Sensei was the last Uchi Deshi of Goju Ryu's founder Miyagi Chojun Sensei. Later they would both train and teach at Sensei Miyazato's dojo the Jundokan.

In 1960 he moved to Tokyo to study commerce at Takushoku University. He was invited to teach at the Yoyogi Dojo. This is where he would teach for the next 15 years. He soon attracted up to 1,000. Even though this was a time of great interest by many students, it was hard time financially. Sensei Higaonna lived in a two tatami mat room and subsisted many times by selling items his mother would send him. Other than a brief job in banking, karate instruction has been Higaonna Sensei's full time occupation.

Students would travel from all over the world to train with him and in 1979 he established the International Okinawan Karate-Do Federation (IOGKF). He has traveled extensively researching the art. He has provided countless hours of instruction and guidance to many karateka all over the world. This being the case, it is remarkable and a compliment to his character that in every encounter this writer has had with him he has been easily approachable, modest and kind.

The Instructors

Sensei Franco Sanguinetti

Sensei Sanguinetti is a very kind man and one of the most qualified martial artists I have ever met. I have studied karate as well as kobudo with him. We are very lucky to be associated with him. The following information about Sensei Sanguinetti can be found on his web site at www.bushikan.com. The pictures in this biography are courtesy of Sensei Sanguinetti.

Sensei Franco Sanguinetti is a descendent of Italian and Spanish grand- parents who migrated to South America after World War II. He began his Budo training in his homeland of Perú, South America, where there is a very extensive Okinawan/Japanese community. Sanguinetti Sensei initiated his training in Budo in 1972, and since then, he has training under the tutelage of strict, traditional Okinawan/Japanese instructors. Many instructors have influenced Sanguinetti's martial arts skills. Among them are well-recognized names such as Higaonna Morio, Kokubo Juichi, Matayoshi Shinpo, and Gakiya Yoshiaki among others.

Although Sensei Sanguinetti holds the rank of Go Dan (5th Dan) in Okinawan Goju Ryu Karate, he has trained and been ranked in Kyokushinkai, Shotokan and Shito Ryu. This exposure to other Karate styles has provided Sensei Sanguinetti with additional knowledge and insight into the martial arts. As a result, he has a more complete understanding of what he does today as the director and chief instructor of the Bushikan Budo Dojo. In addition, he shares his knowledge as a contributing writer to martial arts magazines such as Bugeisha Magazine.

Sanguinetti Sensei's training in Kobudo began parallel to his training in karate, but he did not receive formal training in Matayoshi Kobudo until he moved to Venezuela in 1979. While living in Venezuela, he had the opportunity to meet Hiramatsu Gishin Sensei. Hiramatsu Sensei trained under Matayoshi Shinpo Sensei when the latter was living in mainland Japan. Sensei Sanguinetti met Matayoshi Sensei for the first time in 1981 when he traveled to Okinawa to participate in the 1st IOGKF International Gasshuku & Tournament.

It was during this trip that Sanguinetti Sensei, in search for more depth to his training, made the decision to move to Okinawa, the birthplace of Karate and Kobudo. The following year he moved to Okinawa and trained in three different dojos. He practiced Goju Ryu with Higaonna Sensei, Kobudo with Matayoshi Sensei and Iai-Do with Toyozato Sensei. He fondly refers to that period as the best time in his life because he did not need to focus on anything else other than Budo.

He has competed in national and international tournaments for 13 years, and as a result of his experience in competitions, he has earned positions on prestigious teams such as the Peruvian National Karate Team and the Venezuelan National Karate Team. Sanguinetti Sensei moved permanently to the USA in 1985 where he resides in San Diego, California.

Dojo Etiquette

There is so much involved with etiquette that to the beginner it may seem overwhelming. This is written to get the beginner started and hopefully alleviate some frustration. It does not cover everything but it does cover areas that I feel need to be known right away.

As a beginner, the main thing to remember is that etiquette is not just a robotic act but also an expression of appreciation, kindness and sincerity. If your heart is true, others look at mistakes in etiquette as an opportunity to help and teach you (but please don't mind if you are asked to do push-ups. If you breach etiquette deliberately as an insult, then others may look at this as an opportunity to color you black and blue. Intent is often very obvious in these matters.

1. Juniors arrive early and/or stay late to help clean.
2. Bow and say "Onegai shimasu" when entering the dojo.
3. Bow and say "Domo arigato" when leaving the dojo.
4. Listen to the instructor.
5. Be mindful of the dojo kun.
6. Wear a clean gi.
7. Do not wear jewelry.
8. Do not wear heavy perfumes.
9. Arrive early and warm up on your own before formal class.
10. Keep fingernails and toenails short and clean.
11. Bow when someone hands you training equipment.
12. Do not walk between the instructor and other students.
13. Do not lean on the walls during training.
14. Do not yawn during training.
15. Place your clothing and equipment in order before training.
16. Let senior rank get water first.
17. No shoes on the training floor.
18. Bring water to the instructors.
19. Do not step over equipment or weapons.
20. Leave equipment to the side when not in use.
21. Line up in order of rank. People of the same rank line up by age.
22. Do not leave your belt on the floor.
23. Students are to report any conduct, which is beneath the dignity of the martial arts that they or any other practitioner are engaged in.

Tying the Belt, Standing Bow and Seiza

Tying The Belt

I have counted four different ways of tying a belt, but I will only try to explain the one that Higaonna Sensei uses.

1. First, let the belt hang evenly to find the middle. Take the middle and place it over the center of the waist.
2. Tuck the belt in the right hand under the left side and wrap it around to the front. Take the belt in the left hand and wrap it over to the front and tuck it under all the belts.
3. Next, take this belt end (it is on the left side) and tie it under the end on the right.
4. If done correctly, you should have a triangle pointing from left to right.
5. The belt should make a smooth, straight line across the back both ends should be equal in length.
6. Beginners should practice tying the belt on the heavy bag ten times before each class.

Standing Bow

The bow is a simple yet sincere gesture of respect. It also shows the poise and composure of the person bowing. It is not a humbling gesture. It is done smoothly and in one breath. First, stand in musubi dachi with the hands relaxed and handing naturally by the hips. Then, bow with a straight back to about 25 degree angle, pausing briefly at the end of the extension. Return to the standing position in a fluid manner. The eyes can take in all of the immediate area to guard against attack.

Seiza

Seiza is also a good way to sit quietly. You can cross your feet in back with the right toe over your left toe, or your right foot over your left foot. Women should sit with knees together. Men should sit with knees two fists apart. When bowing, the hands should slide down to the floor at the same time to form a diamond. When leaning forward, your hips should stay low to the ground.

Many basics can be done from this position to isolate the upper body much in the same way Saifa kata isolates the upper body while performing tettsui uchi, strike, grab, pull and ura zuki. Punching and blocking drills can be done from this position. Then you can put them together and add a kick from a half standing position. Some of these types of drills can be done with partners as a yakusoku kumite.

Beginning Vocabulary

Many books have glossaries of terms that are invaluable. However, every student should have a English-Japanese conversion dictionary and *The Overlook Martial Arts Dictionary* by Emil Farakas and John Corcoran (or something similar). Care must be taken to avoid misspellings on some lists, especially those from the internet.

There are several kanji sites on the Internet, which may add to students' breadth of knowledge. One is Jim Breen's Japanese / English Dictionary http://stats.dgim.crc.ca/~jbreen/wwwjdic.html . Another is www.kanjisite.com/wal1.html . For a quick summary of Japanese characters go to www.jun-gifts.com/hanko/explanation.htm. Jeffrey's Japanese English Dictionary is one of the best I have ever seen http://linear.mv.com/cgi-bin/j-e/fg=r/dict .

The Counting, Commands and Essential Expressions section, and the Procedures Before and After Class, of this guidebook will help get students started. Reading through vocabulary lists while taping yourself, and then listening to the tape in the car is a great way to learn vocabulary. So are flash cards. It takes effort but it's worth it!

There is often some confusion on the pronunciation of the word, "*karatedo*." It is four syllables in monotone. There is no emphasis on any of the syllables. *Ka* and *Ra* rhyme and *Te* is pronounced *teh* (not *tay* as in *day*). *Do* is pronounced *doh* (as in bread dough). *Kara* translates as "empty." *Te* translates as "hand" and *Do* translates as "Art." All together *karatedo* translate as the "art of the empty hand." *Goju Ryu* is deliberately not written with a dash (Goju-Ryu or Goju-ryu) in this text. The editorial trend, according to the Japan style Sheet by the Society of Writers, Editors and Translators in Tokyo, is toward eliminating hyphens wherever possible and opting instead for either two separate words or a single word without a hyphen.

Counting

Ichi	1	Ju Ichi	11
Ni	2	Ju Ni	12
San	3	Ju San	13
Shi	4	Ju Shi	14
Go	5	Ju Go	15
Roku	6	Ju Roku	16
Shichi	7	Ju Shichi	17
Hachi	8	Ju Hachi	18
Ku	9	Ju Ku	19
Ju	10	Ni Ju	20

Procedures Before and After Class

The senior student in the dojo calls out these procedures.

Procedure Before Class

Shugo	Line up
Kiyotske	Attention
Seiza	Kneel
Mokuso	Meditation
Mokuso yame	Stop meditation
Shomen ni rei	Bow to front
Sensei ni rei	Bow to teacher
Dozo onegai shimasu (*all say*)	Please teach me
Otagai ni rei	Bow to each other
Dozo onegai shimasu (*all say*)	Please teach me
Tatte	Stand

Procedure After Class

Shugo	Line up
Kiyotske	Attention
Seiza	Kneel
Mokuso	Meditation
Mokuso yame	Stop mediation
Sensei ni rei	Bow to Sensei
Domo arigato gozaimasu (*all say*)	Thank you
Otagai ni rei	Bow to each other
Domo arigato gozaimasu (*all say*)	Thank you
Dojo Jukun (*senior reads*)	(*Class repeats*)
Tatte	Stand

Commands and Essential Expressions

Commands

Yoi	Ready
Hajime	Begin
Mawate	Turn around
Mate	Wait
Yame	Stop
Yasumi	Rest
Hantai	Reverse rotation
Ashi Kaite	Switch legs (sides)
Mo ichi do	One more time

Essential Expressions

Hai	Yes
Iie (sounds like, ee-eye)	No
Arigato	Thank you
Sumimasen	Excuse me
Onegai shimasu	Please help me
Ohayo gozai masu	Good morning
Konnichi wa	Good afternoon
Konban wa	Good evening
Oyasumi nasai	Good night
Sayonara	Good by
Kohai	Junior student
Doshi	Same rank student
Sempai	Senior Student
Sensei	Teacher
Wah-kah-ree- mahs ka?	Do you understand?
Doita shimashite	You are welcome

The Kogen Kan Jukun

Ichi   Strive to develop character and conduct.

Ni   Strive to develop knowledge and abilities.

San   Be self-disciplined, respectful, kind and honest.

Shi   Treat everyone and everything with care.

Go   Maintain balance and flexibility in your life.

Roku   Develop a strong mind, body and indomitable spirit.

Shichi   Push yourself 110% while training.

Hachi   Smile! It'll hurt less. ☺

Ku   Rest and renew.

Ju   Never, ever, ever give up!

The jukun is repeated at the end of class and is used as a reminder for ideals to strive for in daily life. The author developed this jukun. It is hoped that a wide audience will find it useful.

Kanji Corner

These kanji are fun to work with. Often unfamiliar Japanese words can be deciphered by using known kanji and there translations. If you see the kanji for Budo with the last kanji in Shotokan you know the word is *Budo Kan*. These kanji are not exclusively related to Goju Ryu. Having a variety of kanji will help translate more information.

合気道
Aikido

武道
Budo

武士道
Bushido

道場
Dojo

剛柔流
Goju Ryu

範士
Hanshi

居合道
Iaido

柔道
Judo

柔術
Jujutsu

剣道
Kendo

空手道
Karatedo

古武道
Kobudo

沖縄剛柔流
Okinawan Goju Ryu

先輩
Sempai

先生
Sensei

師範
Shihan

糸東流
Shito Ryu

初段
Shodan

松涛館
Shotokan

Phrases

These phrases are common to karate school generally and Goju Ryu school specifically. That is why they have been chosen to be included here.

Ho goju donto: "The Way of inhaling and exhaling is hardness and softness." In proper syntax (Sells,2000) it is, "Ho wa Go Ju o Dan To su" The Law (Ho) includes hardness and softness (or gentle/yin and hard/yang)." This passage is from the *Bubishi*. It may have inspired Chojun Miyagi Sensei as he named Goju Ryu Karate.

Karate ni sente nashi: "There is no first strike in Karate." This is from Gichin Funakoshi Sensei's *Twenty Precepts*. He is widely considered the primary "father" of modern karate due to his efforts to introduce the Okinawan art to mainland Japan and from there it spread to the rest of the world.

Go no sen: Defend and attack. In this situation, you block the opponent's attack and counter attack before he is able to recover from his initial movement.

Sen: Simultaneous attack. In this situation, you and the opponent begin attacking at the same time. Your superior abilities and awareness gives you the advantage.

Sen sen no sen: Interception of attack. In this situation, both people are ready and willing to attack. Your attack must be made in a spilt second between the time the opponent mentally commits to the attack and the moment he begins his actual movement. The opponent's commitment to the attack will prevent him responding with a defense.

Nana korogi, ya oki: Seven times down, eight times up.

Seiryoku zenyo: Maximum effect with minimum effort.

Jita kyoeti: Mutual welfare and benefit.

Zukan soku netsu: Cool head, warm feet.

Hito o mite ho o toke: Change your teaching according to the student.

Hito kata san nen: Three years one kata.

Shuhari: Learning, mastering and transcending tradition.

Shimeijurasan: A state of perfection, which is the goal (albeit unattainable), of martial artists. It is often used to describe perfect kata.

Mizu no Kokoro: Mind like water.

Tsuki no Kokoro: Mind like moon.

Goju Ryu Milestones

These Goju Ryu Milestones are taken from the sources that are noted at the end of this article. Where discrepancies exist, I have tried to reconcile them based on personal research and educated opinions. The largest change that I have made here is to edit out much of the material, aside from some of the earliest dates, that was not directly related to the practice of Goju Ryu. This was done to focus the reader strictly on events concerned with Goju Ryu. These milestones can be studied by partially covering the page, leaving the date visible and trying to recall the information.

475

Bodhidharma arrives in China from India. His legacy is shrouded in legends. He has been credited with many things, from brining tea to China to resurrection. What does not seem to be in dispute is that he taught the monks of a Shaolin Temple the foundations of what evolved into Kung Fu.

1392

The 36 families from China immigrate to Kume village in Naha, Okinawa. Within the settlement, Chinese kempo was practiced.

1477

The ruler King Sho Shin unified the three separate kingdoms of Okinawa. He banned the use of all weapons. This spurred the development of the indigenous self-protection arts of Okinawa.

1609

The Satsuma clan of Japan invaded Okinawa. They met some resistance from the indigenous peoples. This resistance was notable because the Okinawans were seriously outnumbered and outgunned yet they were able to hold there ground to a marked degree. Again, a weapons ban was implemented. This increased the practice of unarmed combat in Okinawa.

1840

Arakaki Seisho Sensei was born. He was the first instructor of Kanryo Higaonna Sensei.

1853

Higaonna Kanryo, founder of Naha-te, was born on March 10th.

Goju Ryu Milestones

1867
At the age of 14, Higaonna Kanryo celebrated katagashira (passage into manhood).

1874
Higaonna Kanryo traveled to Fuzhou China to study Chinese Kempo. He was 22 years old at the time.

1875
After one year in Fuzhou, Higaonna Sensei is introduced to Ryu Ryuko. It was another 4-6 months of chores before he began formal learning. Aragaki Ryuko Sensei is born. He later was Miyagi Sensei's first teacher and introduced him to Kanryo Higaonna Sensei.

1868
This is the beginning of the Meiji Restoration. This was the beginning of the end for the Samurai and Warlord rule.

1882
Kanryo Higaonna Sensei returns from Fuzhou, China and marries on May 15.

1887
Go Kenki was born. He was Chinese and owned a tea store in Naha. Go Kenki was a Hakutsuru ken (white crane fist) master and a very close friend of Miyagi Chojun Sensei. Go Kenki traveled with Miyagi Sensei to China twice to serve as interpreter in 1915 and 1936. Many believe that Go Kenki Sensei taught Miyagi Sensei theory and techniques. He definitely had influence on Miyagi Chojun Sensei's karate; specifically in the development of Tensho kata, which is sometimes called Rokishu. Go Kenki used to teach a kata with the same name.

1888
Miyagi Chojun Sensei, founder of Goju Ryu, was born on April 25th.

Goju Ryu Milestones

1889
Higaonna Kanryo Sensei introduces Naha-te by opening a dojo in Naha.

1896
October 2nd , Itokazu Yoshio founder of Itokazukei Goju Ryu was born.

1898
Higa Seiko Sensei was born. He is the founder of Shodokan Goju Ryu. Both he and Itokanzu Yoshio Sensei are the only two people to train with both Kanryo Higaonna Sensei and Miyagi Sensei. Many believe Higa Seiko Sensei was the most advanced student when Miyagi Sensei died.

1900
Miyagi Chojun Sensei begins training with Aragaki Ryuko.

1901
Shinzato Jinan was born February 5th at Kumemura village in Naha Okinawa. It is accepted by all that he was Miyagi' s chosen successor to Goju Ryu. Interestingly, he is said to have only been taught 3 kata.

1902
Miyagi Chojun Sensei began training with Higaonna Kanryo Sensei. Miyagi Sensei was accepted as a student after having been introduced to Higaonna by Aragaki Ryuko Sensei.

1905
Higaonna Kanryo Sensei began teaching at the Naha Commercial High School.

1908
Takamine Choboku was born on March 24th . Takamine Sensei was a student of Higa Seiko Sensei.

1909
January 20th , Yamaguchi Gogen is born in Kagoshima City, Japan. He was introduced to Miyagi Chojun Sensei by Jitsuei Yogi. Yamaguchi Sensei is the founder of the Japan Goju-kai. It is through Yamaguchi Sensei that Goju Ryu became world known.

Goju Ryu Milestones

1912
Yagi Meitoku Sensei was born on March 6th in Kume-machi, a district in Naha, Okinawa. He is the founder Meibukan Goju Ryu.

1915
May 1915, Miyagi Chojun Sensei and GoKenki journeyed to Fuzhou Province in China in search of Ryu Ryu Ko, and for research. All the information that Miyagi Sensei gathered was lost during WW II. Higaonna Kanryo Sensei dies on December 23rd. Miyagi Chojun Sensei paid for the funeral. Miyagi Chojun Sensei became successor of Naha-te. Miyazato Eiko Sensei was born, founder of Gokenkan Goju Ryu.

1917
Toguchi Seikichi Sensei was born on May 20th in Naha City, Okinawa. Toguchi Sensei was a student of Higa Seiko Sensei and also studied with Miyagi Chojun Sensei. Toguchi Sensei is the founder of Sho-Rei-Kan Goju Ryu.

1918
Arakaki Seisho dies (Alternate death date is 1920)

1919
Fukuchi Seiko was born. He was a student of Higa Seiko Sensei.

1921
Miyagi Chojun Sensei demonstrated Naha-te to Crown Prince Hirohito, who stopped at Okinawa on his way to his European tour.

1922
Miyazato Ei'ichi Sensei, founder of Jundokan Goju Ryu, was born July 5th. Miyagi's family gave Miyazato Sensei all of Miyagi Chojun's hojo undo. Tada Seigo Sensei was born in Kyoto, Japan. One of Yamaguchi Sensei's senior students, Tada Sensei, went on to form the Seigokan organization, which became one of the largest Goju Ryu association in Japan.

1926
Miyagi Chojun Sensei formed the Tode Kenkyukai Club to research and ensure the preservation of the indigenous Okinawa self-protection arts. The co-founders were Hanashiro Chomo, Motobu Choyo and Mabuni Kenwa.

Goju Ryu Milestones

1927
February 10th. Higa Seikichi was born on February 10th . He was one of Higa Seiko's most senior students.

1930
Miyagi Chojun Sensei received an invitation to demonstrate at the all Nippon Budo demonstration to be held on May 5, 1930. Miyagi Sensei sent his senior student Shinzato Jinan Sensei instead. Shinzato performed kata Sanchin and Sesan. It was there that they asked what the name of his style was. Shinzato replied, "Naha-te". Upon his return, Shinzato Jinan Sensei explained to Miyagi Sensei what had happen. Miyagi Chojun named his style Goju Ryu. The name may have been taken from the book *Bubishi*. It reads *"Ho go ju donto"* (See Appendix A) which translates as "the way of inhaling and exhaling is hardness and softness."

1932
Toguchi Seikichi Sensei joined Higa Seiko's Dojo.

1933
Goju Ryu was officially registered with the Dai Nippon Butokukai as a ryu (style). Miyagi Sensei was appointed Chief of Karate for the Okinawan Branch. Miyagi Sensei was awarded the titile Kyoshigo which is the second highest title of the Butokukai.
Anthony Mirakian is born on November 12th . Sensei Mirakian is a senior student of Yagi Meitoku Sensei. According to Yogi Jitsuei Sensei, this was the year that he introduced Yamaguchi Gogen Sensei to Miyagi Chojun Sensei. Yamaguchi Sensei declared that it was 1931.

1934
Miyagi Chojun Sensei lectures and teaches karate in Hawaii.

Goju Ryu Milestones

1935
February, Miyagi Sensei returns from Hawaii. Miyagi Chojun Sensei give a demonstration in mainland Japan, with Jitsuei Sensei as his assistant. The Toudi (karate) Kenkyukai (research club) was formed on December 21st. Sensei John Roseberry, founder of Sho Rei Sho Bu Kan Goju Ryu, was born on March 8th. Yamaguchi Gogen founded the All Japan Goju-Kai association. Peter Urban founder of USA Goju is born on August 14th. Yamaguchi Gosei is born on January 15th in Kyoto.

1936
Miyagi Sensei presents the *"Outline of Karatedo"* in Osaka.

1938
Shinjo Masanobu, founder of Shobukan Goju Ryu is born. Shinjo Sensei was the Chief Instructor of Toguchi Seikichi Sensei's Sho Rei Kan. Shinjo Sensei went to many of Miyagi's top students to learn the kata they had been taught by Miyagi Sensei. Higaonna Morio, founder of the International Organization of Goju Ryu Karatedo Federation (IOGKF) is born on December 25th.

1939
Yamaguchi Sensei travels to Manchuria as an intelligence officer.
The Dai Nihon Butokukai awarded Jinan Shinzato Sensei the title *Renshi*.

1940
Miyagi Chojun Sensei and Nagamine Shoshin Sensei (founder of Matsubayashi Shorin Ryu) created the Gekisai kata to popularize and standardize karate. These kata are aggressive in nature and were used to prepare students for war thus the last move is forward in Gekisai Dai Ichi.

1941
Chinen Teruo Sensei was born.

1942
Miyagi Sensei is invited to teach at Ritsumei Kan University in Kyoto. A person offered to buy rank from him so he never retuned.

Goju Ryu Milestones

1944
October 10th, Americans attack Okinawa.
Hokama Tetushiro, a student of Higa Seiko Sensei and Fukuchi Seiko Sensei was born.

1945
Shinzato Jinan dies during the battle of Okinawa.
Emperor Hirohito surrenders.

1947
Yamaguchi Sensei returns from China. Miyagi Sensei begins teaching at the Naha Police Academy.

1950
Yamaguchi Sensei forms the Karatedo Goju Kai in Tokyo.

1951
Miyagi Sensei begins accepting some students at his home to train in his garden. Miyagi An'ichi Sensei (no family relation to Chojun Miyagi Sensei) and Aragaki Suichi Sensei were the only two training consistently before this.

1953
Miyagi Chojun dies on October 8th at the age of 65.

1955
Toguchi Sensei opened first Sho Rei Kan Dojo in Koza City Okinawa. Joe White is the first American to train with Toguchi Sensei.

1956
Joe White introduces Roseberry Sensei to Toguchi Sensei.
Higaonna Morio Sensei begins training at the garden dojo.

1957
Miyazato Ei'ichi established Jundokan Dojo. Miyagi An'ichi, Higaonna Morio, Chinen Teruo and Uehara Ko all trained at Miyazato's Jundokan Dojo

Goju Ryu Milestones

1958

Joe White is the first non-Asian to receive an instructors certificate from Taguchi Sensei.

1959

Peter Urban introduces Japanese Goju Ryu to the United States.
Jack Coleman Sensei, a student of Izumikawa Sensei, begins teaching Goju Ryu in the Midwest.

1960

Anthony Mirakian brings Meibukan Goju Ryu to the United States. He is 9th Dan, Meibukan's highest ranking non-Asian.

1961

Hokama Sensei begins training with Higa Seiko Sensei at Naha Commercial High School.

1962

Gosen Yamaguchi Sensei, the son of Yamaguchi Sensei, begins teaching Goju Kai at the University of San Francisco.

1963

Yagi Meitoku receives from Miyagi family Miyagi Chojun Sensei's gi and belt. However, Miyazato Ei'ichi purchased this gi and belt as a gift for Miyagi Sensei. Miyazato bought it while in Japan, when he went to compete in Judo.
Yamguchi Sensei joins his son in America.
In California, Rodney Hu Sensei becomes a San Dan and a Chief Instructor under Yamaguchi Sensei. Prior to this, in Hawaii, Hu Sensei was a student of Oshiro Sensei who was the Goju Kai representative there. Hu Sensei opens a dojo in Stockton, California.
Sensei John S. O'Hara begins training in Naha-Te.

1964

Bill Reuter Sensei, a student of Oshiro Sensei, begins teaching Goju Kai in Reno, Nevada.

Goju Ryu Milestones

1966
Higa Seiko dies. Peter Urban founds USA Goju. Hokama Tetsuhiro continued his training with Fukuchi Seiko Sensei.
Oshiro Sensei receives the rank of Go Dan from Yamaguchi Sensei.

1967
Sensei John S. O'Hara converts to Goju Kai and combines dojo in Bakersfield, California with Sandy Chaddick and Jack Griffin.

1968
Sensei Mike Mancuso (presently an 8th Dan) brings Jundokan Goju Ryu to the United States. Roseberry Sensei begins teaching in Lincoln Nebraska. Tomano Sensei and Ong Sensei begin teaching in New York. Tamano Sensei is a student of Toguchi Sensei and Ong is a student of Kawakami Sensei.

1969
Chinen Teruo Sensei, a student of Miyazato Ei'ichi Sensei (Jundokan Goju Ryu), introduces Okinawa Goju Ryu to Spokane, Washington.

1973
Sensei Ron Van Clief, a student of Sensei Peter Urban and Sensei Frank Ruiz, forms his own system called Chinese Goju.

1979
Higaonna Morio Sensei leaves Miyazato Ei'ichi Sensei and forms the International Okinawan Goju Ryu Karate-Do Federation (IOGKF).

1983
Shinjo Sensei leaves Toguchi Sensei and Sho Rei Kan organization and formed the Shobukan Dojo. Sensei Roseberry parts from the Sho Rei Kan and forms the Sho Rei Shobu Kan in honor of Toguchi and Shinjo sensei.

1988
Higaonna Sensei opens the IOGKF Honbu Dojo in San Marcos California. Sensei Franco Sanguinetti moves his students to Higaonna's dojo. Sensei Sanguinetti is Sempai of Honbu Dojo.

Goju Ryu Milestones

1989
Yamaguchi Gogen dies on May 20th.
His oldest son Gosei takes over America Goju Kai, and his youngest son Goshi runs Goju Kai International.

1993
Shinjo Masanobu Sensei dies on October 15th.

1994
Kina Seiko dies.

1997
Shihan John Roseberry receives 9th Dan from the United States Karate Alliance (USKA).

1998
Toguchi Seikichi dies on August 31st at the age of 81.

1999
Miyazato Ei'ichi Sensei dies.

Sources:

The Goju Ryu Homepage. Retrieved December 12, 2002 from
http://gojuryu.net/

Okinawa Goju Ryu Karate-Jutsu Kenkyukai. Retrieved November 16, 2001 from
http://www.naha-te.com/

Sells, J. (2000) *Unante The Secrets of Karate 2nd Edition* Hollywood: W.H. Hawley Publishing (the first Limited Edition was published in 1995)

Wilson, Steven R. (1998) *The Manuscript of Okinawan Goju Ryu* This was given to this writer by it's author in 1998. It is a 74 page unpublished work that is not available to the general public.

Meet the Masters

東恩納寛量先生
Higaonna Kanryo Sensei

Born: 1853
Died: 1915
Studied Under:
Seisho Arakaki Sensei
Ryu Ryuko Sifu

Some Contributions Include:
Brought back
 Sanchin, Saifa, Seiyunchin,
 Shisochin, Seipai, Kururunfa,
 Sesan and Suparinpei from
 China.
Founded Naha-Te.
Taught in public schools.

Some Top Students Include:
Miyagi Chojun Sensei
Juhatsu Kiyoda Senei
Kenuwa Mabuni

宮城長順先生
Miyagi Chojun Sensei

Born: 1888
Died: 1953
Studied Under:
Aragaki Ryuko Sensei
Kanryo Higaonna Sensei

Some Contributions Include:
Developed Junbi Undo.
Created Gekisai Kata with
 Shoshine Nagamine.
Developed Tensho Kata and a
 revised version of Sanchin.
Introduced Goju Ryu to Hawaii
 and Japan.
Named the Style Goju Ryu.

Some Top Students Include:
Jin'an Shinzato
Seko Higa
Yoshio Itokanzu
Sekichi Toguchi
Meitoku Yagi
Ei'ichi Miyazato
An'ichi Miyagi

Chapter 1: The Kogen Kan

Meet the Masters

Ei'ichi Miyazato Sensei:

Born: 1921
Died: 1999

Studied Under:
Miyagi Chojun Sensei
Jigoro Kano Sensei (Judo)

Some Contributions Include:
Established the Jundokan
  Organization.
Ranked Morio Higaonna Sensei
  to 6th Dan.
Ranked An'ichi Miyagi Sensei.

Some Top Students Include:
Ko Uehara
Masafumi Suzuki
Ryosei Aragaki
Seikichi Kinjo
Saburo Higa
Nanko Minei

Seko Higa Sensei

Born: 1889
Died: 1966

Studied Under:
Kanryo Higaonna Sensei
Miyagi Chojun Sensei

Some Contributions Include:
Taught in Saipan for two years.
Established Shodokan
  Goju Ryu.

Some Top Students Include:
Seikichi Higa (his son)
Choboku Takamine
Seiyu Nakasone
Seiko Kina
Seiko Fukuchi
Kanki Isumikawa
Jui Tamaki
Tomoshige Yohena
Toyohide Taira
Hoshu Taira
Choshin Ishamine
Mitsugi Kobayashi

Meet the Masters

Meitoku Yagi Sensei

Born: 1912
Died: 2003
Studied Under:
Miyagi Chojun Sensei

Some Contributions Include:
Established the Meibukan
  Organization.

Some Top Students Include:
Meitatsu Yagi (son)
Meitetsu Yagi (son)
Shigetoshi Seneha
Anthony Merakian
Yasuaki Hokama
Masanao Miyazato
Junbin Seneha
Seiko Nakamoto
Yasunori Yonamine

Gogen Yamaguchi Sensei

Born: 1909
Died: 1989
Studied Under:
Yogi Jitsuei
Miyagi Chojun Sensei

Some Contributions Include:
Formed the Goju Kai
  Organization.
Established Jiyu Kumite.
Expanded Taikioku Kata.
Expanded Kihon Ido.

Some Top Students Include:
Gosei Yamaguchi (his son)
Goshi Yamagughi (his son)
Gosen Yamaguchi (his son)
Shozo Ujita
Tomoharu Kisaki
Kenzo Uchiage
Haruyoshi Kagawa
Tada Seigo

Meet the Masters

Seikichi Toguchi Sensei:

Born: 1917
Died: 1998

Studied Under:
Miyagi Chojun Sensei
Higa Seko

Some Contributions Include:
Founded Sho Rei Kan.
Created continuous bunkai.
Created Kakuha Katas 1 and 2.
Created Hookiyu Katas 1 and 2.

Top Students Include:
Shinjo Masanobu
Katsuyoshi Kanei
Yoshio Shimabuku
Akira Kawakami
Yoshinori Higa
Toshio Tamano
Ryugo Sakai
Choyu Kyuna
Kinei Nakasone
Anthony Mirakian
Joe White
John Roseberry

An'ichi Miyagi Sensei:

Born: 1931
Died: ----

Studied Under:
Miyagi Chojun Sensei as his last
Uchi Deshi

Some Contributions Include:
Taught at the Miyagi Sensei's
Garden Dojo after Miyagi
Sensei's Death.
Taught at the Jundokan.

Top Students Include:
Morio Higaonna

All of these Master's vital information can be studied by partially covering up the data with a piece of paper and quizzing yourself as you slide the paper down the page.

Goju Ryu Lesson Plan

Date _____

Junbi Undo _____

_____

Hojo Undo _____

_____

Kihon and Kihon Ido _____

_____

Renzoku and Taikyoku _____

_____

Kata and Bunkai _____

_____

Kakie _____

_____

Kotei Ate _____

_____

Kumite _____

_____

Other _____

    This Goju Ryu Lesson Plan page can be reproduced and completed prior to each class. It is useful to note a few specifics in each area to be taught. Having these lesson plans to review will insure that over a period of time the entire curriculum will be covered.

Invitation to Test

WHITE BELT

10. Ju Kyu	White Belt (Min. age of 10)
9. Ku Kyu	One stripe
8. Hachi Kyu	Two stripes
7. Shichi Kyu	Three stripes

GREEN BELT

6. Roku Kyu	One stripe
5. Go Kyu	Two stripes
4. Yon Kyu	Three stripes

BROWN BELT

3. San Kyu	One stripe
2. Ni Kyu	Two stripes
1. Ik Kyu	Three stripes

BLACK BELT

1. Shodan One year Ik Kyu (Min. age 16)	2. Nidan 3. Sandan 4. Yondan (Renshi)	5. Godan (Kyoshi) 6. Rokudan (Shihan)	7. Nanadan 8. Hachidan 9. Kyudan (Hanshi)	10. Judan

There is a six month duration between kyu ranking. This is a minimum time requirement for grading and is based on regular class attendance in addition to out of class effort.

Please realize that you can decline to grade if you wish. It is also important to know that grading is as much for the examiners as it is for the students. Gradings help the examiners know what is working and what needs more work. Grading will be held at the end of January and the end of July.

Black belt minimum time requirements follow this pattern: Nidan, two years of Shodan; Sandan, three years of Nidan; Yondan, four years of Sandan etc. Black belt grading will be in front of a grading panel. The panel will set minimum age requirements.

Name: _____

Current Rank: _____ Testing Rank: _____

Date of Test: _____ Time of Test: _____

Comments: _____

Grading Rubric

Student _____ Date _____

Current Rank _____ Testing Rank _____

Examiner _____ Comments↓

Junbi Undo	0	1	2	3	4	5 _____
Kihon	0	1	2	3	4	5 _____
Kihon Ido	0	1	2	3	4	5 _____
Hojo Undo	0	1	2	3	4	5 _____
Kakie	0	1	2	3	4	5 _____
Kotei Ate	0	1	2	3	4	5 _____
Renzoku	0	1	2	3	4	5 _____
Kata	0	1	2	3	4	5 _____
Bunkai	0	1	2	3	4	5 _____
Kumite	0	1	2	3	4	5 _____
Focus Shields	0	1	2	3	4	5 _____
Mental Endurance	0	1	2	3	4	5 _____
Physical Endurance	0	1	2	3	4	5 _____
Vocabulary	0	1	2	3	4	5 _____
Character and Conduct	0	1	2	3	4	5 _____

Written
Requirement Done?   Yes   No   NA _____

Overall Comments: _____

_____

_____

With a score of ten, "5's" or more, a student may be allowed to advance two grades. Students must retake all or part of the exam if a student scores a, "0" in any category. The student may have to retake all or part of the exam if a score is less than, "2" in any category. The range is 0=Retest, 1=Poor, 2=Fair, 3= Good, 4=Very Good, 5=Excellent

Grading Record

Name	Ju Kyu	Ku Kyu	*Hachi Kyu*	*Shichi Kyu*	*Roku Kyu*	*Go Kyu*	*Yon Kyu*	San Kyu	*Ni Kyu*	*Ik Kyu*	*Shodan*

Instructors can keep this as a quick reference of student progress. Names and grading dates can be written in as needed.

Chapter 1: The Kogen Kan

The Kogen Kan

Notes

Chapter 2

Junbi Undo

Chapter 2 Table of Contents

Introduction

Junbi Undo are exercises which prepare the body for Karate training. Miyagi Chojun Sensei developed them with the assistance of a doctor of acupuncture. I believe the original spirit and intent of Miyagi Sensei was to provide a good warm up to prevent injuries, develop flexibility, and build endurance and strength. This may not seem revolutionary now, but at the time it was virtually unique. It was an indication of Miyagi Sensei's forward thinking and overall expertise.

It is my opinion that much has been changed, by additions or deletions, since he originally developed junbi undo. I believe this is because instructors have their favorite junbi undo that they emphasize. It is equally true that, consciously or not, instructors have junbi undo that they do not emphasize. Much of Miyagi Sensei's original writings were lost in the war so it is difficult to tell what he did with absolute certainty.

Much of what is written here is derived from Higaonna Sensei's books and tapes. These are probably the closest to the original junbi undo as he has trained with two of Miyagi Sensei's direct students.

Every student is encouraged to do more research. Other junbi undo are provided with special emphasis on the push-up.

On a final note, the performance of junbi undo can be thought of as similar to the performance of kata. So focus. Look for self-defense techniques in the junbi undo. You will be pleasantly surprised.

Traditional Junbi Undo

1. Toe exercises 2. Ankle rotation/press 3. Ankle stretches (go out on sokuto with both feet -opposite- then rock side to side -same direction) 4. Heel to toe rock 5. Knee bends 6. Knee bends with circles 7. Knee bends outside, inside 8. One leg extended out to side while sitting on opposite foot and zenkutsu dachi stretch 9. Touch toes and then lean back doing each side individually 10. Rotation of whole body like a windmill 11. Rotate hips 12. Leg raises forward and crossing at 45 degrees touching extended hand each time 13. Knee strikes 14. Ushiro Geri, yoko geri, mawashi geri, mae geri 15. Mika zuki geri (can be done with a partner who ducks under and counters) 16. Backward stretching leaning back and exhaling 17. Tora guchi side to side, back and down 18. Shiko dachi, grab ankles and press looking left and right 19. Shiko dachi one and two hand press to sky also grabbing backward 20. Neko undo pushups (downward dog, down, head right, head left, head down, downward dog, cat stretch, downward dog) 21. Donkey kicks 22. Squat kicks 23. Butterfly kicks 24. Sin yings 25. Swing one arm individually switch, then rotating both arms together big and small circles (all done front and back) 26. Chest pulls 27. Finger press 28. Neck stretches looking left and right, rotations, ear to shoulder 29. Scissors kicks 30. Neck down and back harmonized with breathing (breathing out when going down and back, in while going to center) 31. Neck rotations (slowly) 32. Two person stretches, standing side to side and facing each other with legs apart

Additional Junbi Undo

1. Two partners back to back hook arms, sit down, extend legs, stand up 2. Fireman carry with partner or heavy bag and do squats 3. Sit-ups to standing position while partner holds legs 4. Leg wrestling 5. Neck exercises, bridges and lifting head while laying on focus shields 6. Two person chest pulls 7. Sin Yings ten on one side, ten in the middle, ten on the other side 8. Frog hops 9. Sprints 10. Running in place and push-ups 11. Backward bicycle 12. Jump rope 13. Leg lifts 14. Jumping jacks (intermittent, fast then slow then fast, with turning back, left right, front, dropping and doing push-ups, arm circles, chest pulls, moving right to left, single arm circles, with ankle weights and hand weights) 15. Eyes (left, right, up, down) 16. Inverted military press 17. One partner on back, the other on his feet. The partner on the floor pushes the partner hard away with his feet. This can be done slowly and with one person on each leg 18. Right leg behind left, go up on calf, switch 19. Right leg behind left and go down in one legged squat 20. Crunches 21. Partner curl-ups 22. Supermen 23. Crab walk 24. Army crawl 25. Hop on one foot up and down the floor 26. Lift one leg and rotate hip as in mawashi geri. Twist the supporting foot to move up and down the floor 27. From a position similar to a push-up move, your legs as if you are running in place 28. One partner takes off his belt, loops it through another's and provides resistance as the person wearing the belt tries to do gyaku zuki in zenkutsu dachi.

Push Ups

1. Hold one pushup for 5 minutes (can be done one handed) 2. Partner push-ups (one partner on all fours, the other with his legs on top) 3. Diamond 4. Wide 5. Knuckle 6. Wrist 7. Finger 8. One arm (or hold for 5 minutes) 9. Up one count, middle two count, down three count 10. "T" push up (three people do together, one in middle has both partners legs on top, switch) 11. Shuto 12. Medicine ball (individually or with a pair) 13. Table or chair push-ups 14. Tonfa or Chishi push-ups 15. Finger push-ups from five down to two 16. On knees 17. Inchworm push-ups 18. Bo push-ups (hands on both sides of a bo then switch 19. Clapping push-ups 20. In line push-ups (partners feet on others shoulders) 21. Knuckle push-ups but face the fist like a punch 22. Have a partner place his fist underneath your chest. Only count the push-ups that touch the fist 23. Do a push-up then flip to face up, dip, then flip to face down, do a push-up then flip face up the other direction, repeat 24. Wheelbarrow races with push-ups 25. Countertop push-ups 26. Clapping push-ups with fists (tate zuki and seiken zuki) 27. Partners can keep a focus pad between their foreheads while they go from standing, to push-ups and back to standing, without dropping the focus pad. 28. Have a partner place weights on the back of the person doing push-ups.

Junbi Undo

Notes

Chapter 3

Hojo Undo

Chapter 3 Table of Contents

Introduction

This contains notes that are to serve as reminders. These were written so they could be easily posted in the dojo. Many of these notes will only make sense with proper instruction. This is only a tool to help in retention of that instruction and is not a substitute for it. I encourage everyone to do their own research, including making their own hojo undo, to add to this fund of knowledge. Be safe and have fun!

Hojo Undo Identification

Chishi: These can be made by inserting screw into a dowel and placing it into a coffee can or a plastic flowerpot then filling it with concrete.

Focus Shield: These usually cost about $40. Kids can use couch cushions if these are too hard.

Heavy Bag: Come in a variety of weights and coverings. A comfortable weight is often 60 lbs. Vinyl can be cleaned easily. If it is hung horizontally, it is a good target for keage geri and hiza geri.

Ishi Sashi: This can be awkward to make. Sometimes, manufactured weights have a curved handle over the bar that works as well.

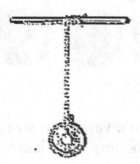

Kigu Makiage: These are easy to make with a bar, rope and weight.

Hojo Undo Identification

Kongoken: This can be made by using four 90° electrical conduit and two straight pieces of the same. Before they are welded together, each section is capped with a disk on one end, filled with sand and then caped with a disk on the other end.

Makiwara: The makiwara should move 2-4 inches when being hit. Any less and it may be too hard, thus resulting in back injuries. Any more and it will not be useful in conditioning the body.

Medicine Ball: These come in a variety of sizes. The leather type is best for punching and kicking.

Hojo Undo Identification

Nigiri Game: These were originally made of ceramic and many broke. Now there are some made of pipes, plastic jars and even hex-weights can be used.

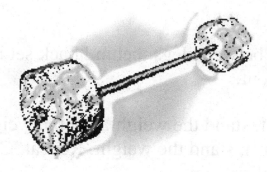

Tan: The tan shown here is made of wood and concrete much like a two sided Chishi. There is something to be said for using natural materials to make implements; however, iron weights work well too.

Chishi

1. Triceps- weight behind head, arm bent back and lifting up.

2. Biceps- fist under elbow, lifting weight in arm bend.

3. Punching- one hand holding weight and doing gyaku zuki.

4. Both hands holding weight, dropping into shiko dachi (45°) and thrusting.

5. Blocks- moving weight held by opposite hand with forearm while blocking chudan hiki uke, then turn it upside down and do the same thing.

6. Swing weight between legs, behind back set into shiko dachi and grip in then out.

7. Dip the weight, stand the weight, roll the weight by dipping it around the forearm, stand the weight. Repeat. Can be done while dropping into shiko dachi.

8. Make an "X" shape as you would with a sword.

9. Tate zuki.

10. a) Lift over head and back stop front b) Lift down and back stop front.

<u>*Chishi*</u>

11. Swing all the way around body and then stand the Chishi (do in both directions.)

12. Two handgrip, lift behind head and back to front. Twist in then twist out dropping into shiko dachi. Stand and bring back in, turn upside down, twist out dropping into shiko dachi.

13. Shiko dachi gripping weight upside down, twist out then in, keeping back straight, bend and push through legs bring back to chest, look up, straighten up, switch hand and repeat.

14. Osae uke training-handle inside and twist down.

15. Baseball bat swing shifting zenkutsu dachi.

16. Wood choppers strike.

17. Turn upside down and use for pushups.

18. Some may be turned upside down and used as nigiri game.

19. Grip stone weight end and drop into shiko dachi while striking up.

20. Chishi can be used for body conditioning individually and with partners.

21. Heito strike

Focus Shield

The focus shields always win. They are one of the toughest workouts around. They can be used individually or as a pair. There are weak spots to the focus shield that can be minimized if they are hit on the logo in the middle. Holding the focus shield can be difficult and one needs to hold it tight and close to the body. Don't let the elbow stick out because it may hit the kicker's foot.

Focus Shield Drills

1. All punches (see makiwara).
2. All kicks.
3. Some blocks.
4. Combinations of kicks and punches.
5. Renzoku.
6. Freestyle for endurance.
7. Have students lay on the ground and kick away as you attack holding the focus shield.

Three Person Drills

1. One person stand in front, one in back, practice kicking mae geri and ushiro geri against two attackers.
2. Two people stand 45° and the person in middle practices tai sabaki, alternating kicking the bags with mawashi geri.
3. Strike facing forward in zenkutsu gyaku zuki, then turn 45° and strike facing that direction in zenkutsu dachi.
4. Freestyle for endurance.

Small Forearm Focus Shield Drills

1. The holder moves the small focus shields and calls out the technique to do. The common techniques uses are jabs, cross, mawashi geri and hiza geri.
2. The same as number one but with sweeping by the other focus shield to make the attacker duck, bob and weave.
3. While one person blocks the other pounds with the focus shields. This gives resistance to the blocks and improves muscle development. The pounder can call out the blocks.
4. The same as number three only with one block and counter.

Heavy Bag

The heavy bag can be used to develop powerful hitting and kicking. Two people can often work on the bag together. Smaller heavy bags can be used much the same as medicine balls. The heavy bag can be used as a weight bench and gives great support and range of motion while bench pressing. One kicking drill to develop the top of the foot is to place the heavy bag on the floor and have two people kick it at the same time with opposite feet so that is stays in one place. When the bag is hanging, it is useful to put on kumite gear and do one-minute rounds in preparation for sparring.

Heavy Bag Drills:

1. Kicking mawashi geri with one leg all the way around the bag and back, then change legs.

2. Placing the ankle weights on the wrists (along with padded hand gear) to add weight and develop arms.

3. Kicking the bag from underneath as a groin kick.

4. Strike the bag along the vertical axis all the way up and down using a variety of techniques such as age zuki, seiken zuki and furi zuki.

5. Two people can kick or hit the heavy bag at the same time if they are timing things carefully.

6. The heavy bag can be used to develop sweeps and kakato geri if it is on the ground.

7. Kihon can be done on the bag for balance.

8. Hiza geri can be done on the bag up and down the floor.

9. With the bag lying on a thick mat, jump over the bag and execute a given technique. This drill focuses on landing, setting and striking quickly. The strikes can be done against a focus shield.

Ishi Sashi

Opening: Inhale and exhale three times while holding the ishi sashi at the sides in heiko dachi, then open as in Shisochin kata.

1. Slowly pull back and punch, gripping the hand into a fist and rolling it over. Repeat with sanchin stepping.

2. Drop into shiko dachi, grasping firmly as you raise the wrists upwards in morote hara uke.

3. Raise arms straight out to the sides of the shoulders. Bend the elbows and bring the ishi sashi to the front of the face as you drop into shiko dachi, repeat by raising and brining the arms straight out to the shoulders again.

4. Tate zuki.

5. Kicks: mae geri, kansetsu geri, etc.

6. Leg rises similar to hiza geri.

According to Higaonna Sensei on the *Panther Production* tape, in days past, the ishi sashi were thrown up and caught on the elbow. They were also tossed between people. These exercises became rare as karate began to be practiced mainly indoors. Research into how these exercises were done needs to be carried out.

Kigu Makiage

The kigu is a weight attached to a bar by a rope. The weight is rolled up and down to build strength in the forearms. The kigu can also be used with one hand by quickly flicking the wrist and rolling the weight up that way. The kigu can be done while in every stance and while moving in stances. Moving in stances tends to keep your mind off the burn. Resting the forearms on the back of a chair can reduce some of the pressure on the shoulders. The kigu can be used with the arms facing up and then facing down.

<u>Kongoken</u>

The kongoken is a large oval weight that was presented to Miyagi Chojun Sensei while he was in Hawaii. Dimensions can vary. The one I am most familiar with is 88 pounds, 5 feet high and 2 feet wide. The oval weight can scar the floor so the proper surface is necessary for its use. This usually is a thick rubber mat or carpet.

<u>Kongoken Exercises</u>

1. Moving in shiko dachi and neko dachi with it over shoulders.

2. Passing the kongoken to your partner after shifting in heiko dachi.

3. Sawing the ground.

4. Twisting the kongoken while shifting back and forth in heiko dachi.

5. Thrusting the kongoken back and forth while one end stays on the ground.

6. Leg press. One partner lays on the floor and places the kongoken on his feet. The other partner places his weight on the kongoken while the partner on the floor does leg presses.

7. Sit-ups while raising the kongoken above the head. This can be done with partners or alone.

8. Hang the kongoken from your wrists horizontally then flip it over onto your forearms.

9. Body conditioning by pivoting the kongoken on its end and swinging it so it hits your shoulder and forearm.

10. Catch the kongoken on the forearms while passing it back and forth with a partner.

11. Push-ups with the kongoken on your neck.

Makiwara

1. Oi zuki

2. Gyaku zuki

3. Uraken uchi (back to makiwara)

4. Shotei zuki

5. Mawashi hiza geri

6. Heiko dachi, mae geri, oi zuki

7. Hiji ate

8. Yoko ko uke

9. Gedan hara zuki (shifting into shiko dachi)

10. Chudan yoko uke (forearm)

11. Uchi uke

12. Mae geri hiji ate

13. Morote zuki

14. Kagi zuki

15. Haito zuki

16. Shuto (front and back)

17. Open back hand conditioning

18. Sun zuki (one inch punch)

19. Nakadaka ippon ken

20. Ushiro geri

21. Tate zuki

22. Kizami zuki

23. Hiza geri (nihon)

Note: Two people can use the makiwara at one time by using opposite hands and taking turns. Experimentation with shifting and turning is encouraged.

Medicine Ball

The medicine ball can vary in weight from 9-12 pounds. The size increases slightly with the weight. The medicine ball can be leather and filled with sand or it can have a rubber exterior with some heavy filling. My preference is the leather variety. It is not as durable but it is more forgiving and can be punched and kicked without reservation. The leather variety is also better for body conditioning. Each toss can be caught with the body to develop the ability to take a punch. Care must be taken to not strain the lower back when performing medicine ball exercises. Self-regulation is necessary.

Medicine Ball Exercises

1. Throwing like a soccer ball to partner's chest.

2. Thrusting like a bullet-pass (like in basketball) to partner's chest.

3. Thrusting like a bullet-pass to partner's chest followed by a punch (possibly gyaku zuki, alternating hands).

4. Thrusting like a bullet pass to partner's chest followed by a kick (possibly mawashi geri).

5. Thrusting around in a group (if you drop it ten push ups).

6. One partner (standing) throws the ball to the person doing sit-ups who catches it and throws it back after doing a sit up.

7. One partner does a sit-up with the medicine ball and the other partner hits it as they come up together with legs locked (ten each side).

8. Lift legs while holding the medicine ball between ankles and hold.

9. Lock legs with both partners down for sit-ups and passing the ball back and forth.

10. Pass the ball around a group standing with backs together.

Chapter 3: Hojo Undo

Nigiri Game

In *Traditional Karate-Do Okinawan Goju Ryu Volume 1* (Higaonna, 1985), and the *Traditional Okinawan Goju Ryu Karate-Do* (Panther Production, 1981) videotape only shows basic Sanchin stepping while lifting the nigiri game to the front and side (individually and together). The Tsunami Video *Power Training* (1994) tape shows the same movements in shiko dachi and neko dachi. A synopsis of these references and some additional ideas are listed here.

1. Always begin by bowing, assuming sanchin dachi, dipping straight down and grasping the nigiri game and standing straight up.

2. Always bend the thumb, face the seiken knuckles forward and pull the nigiri game up toward the palm. The arms should be up and back.

3. Perform three points of kime:
        a. One at the beginning just after the step.
        b. One at the high point of the lift.
        c. One after coming back to the beginning.

4. Movements from kata can be done. This is probably some of the best training. For example:
        a. Moving in zenkutsu dachi and morote zuki (or lifting) as in Gekisai Dai Ichi.
        b. Morote zuki as in Saifa.
        c. Archer block and mountain block and role from Seiyunchin.
        d. Shotei zuki and arm bar as in Shisochin.
        e. Morote ko uke as in Sanseru (this can be done while in Sanchin Dachi, stepping and switching which hand is on top).

Tan

The bar, the bar with weights (tan), and dumbbells will be addressed inclusively here.

The bar: The bar can be used to practice mawashi uke, bo techniques military press and twisting the hips in shiko dachi. Body conditioning can be done by letting the bar roll down the forearms, catching it at the wrist and tossing it back up.

The bar with weights: The bar with weights can be used to bench press and to do curls. They also can hold feet for sing yings. Abdominal exercises can be done by kneeling and rolling the bar with weights in and out, to the left, middle and right.

Dumbbells: Dumbbells can be used while performing blocks and punches. Curls can be done by placing one fist under the curling elbow and raising the dumbbell, being careful to twist strongly to the outside as in chudan yoko uke. Kata can be done with dumbbells but only after a person is at the green belt level so that the muscles don't become accustomed to poor positioning. Hexagon dumbbells may be used as nigiri game if they are turned on end.

Hojo Undo

Notes

Chapter 4

Kihon

Chapter 4 Table of Contents

Kihon

General Introduction

Kihon is a fundamental part of karate training. Every time I revisit kihon I learn something new. It never ceases to amaze me.

Translated, kihon means "basic." But don't let the term fool you. This term means basic in the sense of, "forming the base or essence." It does not mean, "simple".

All kihon must be practiced in every stance. Kihon can also be practiced while shifting (tai sabaki) in various stances side-to-side, front to back, and at 45° angles. Kihon can be practiced either turning or facing different directions (like kata) to give the ability of transference. If kihon is done slowly, as in Sanchin kata, then shime can be given to prepare students for Sanchin kata. Kihon can be practiced by alternating from a stance with one foot, to the same stance with the other foot.

Combinations of kihon techniques can be practice as in Kihon Ni and San, first just standing, then with sabaki. The shifting can be done side to side, at diagonals, and turning can be done as well. This helps develop continuous fighting techniques.

All kihon can also be done as moving drills, known as Kihon Ido (both forward and backward), in every stance, and on focus shields. The Neko Ashi Kihon focuses on neko ashi to reinforce this particular stance.

It has been said that there are no advanced techniques in karate. Only the performance of the technique makes it beginning, intermediate or advanced; therefore, this kihon section is not classified in that type of levels. However, this Kihon Chapter is modeled, almost verbatim, after Morio Higaonna's *Traditional Okinawan Goju Ryu Karate-Do* (1981, Panther Production) videotapes, specifically Volumes 3,4,5 and 6. This was done so that they could be used as video companions for this section of the guidebook. This being said, I still believe there is great value and importance to learning in a dojo and emulating a qualified teacher.

Stances

Introduction

Different people have different sizes and shapes; therefore, the stances will need to be customized for each person. A tall, light person may need to have a longer zenkutsu dachi with more weight on the front leg in order to deliver punches with power.

Stances have been standardized for teaching purposes; however, students are encouraged to look at what is best for them. It is important to keep some things in mind during this process. The soles of the feet need to grip the floor and the knees need to be flexed. The hips are used for power when delivering techniques. The shoulders are relaxed.

Almost all of the stances in Goju Ryu Karate are training stances. They are used to develop power, balance, and speed. In combat, stances are fluid and dynamic. You no longer focus on sticking the feet to the floor. The stances change quickly and naturally. This is known as Tai Sabaki.

It has been said that when Miyagi Chojun Sensei would first teach kata, he would first teach hand positions and the directions of the eyes only. Once these had been learned, he would teach stances according to the person's body weight and size.

It is always important to focus on the soles of the feet and keep the legs flexed. In kumite, you no longer focus this way but it should come naturally when delivering a technique. Raising and lowering in stances telegraphs your technique.

Stances

Stances

Heisoku Dachi: Closed Foot Stance, as used in Shisochin Kata. The legs bend as the technique is delivered.

Musubi Dachi: Attention Stance, used in the yoi position. Focus on the big toe and the inner-underside of the foot sole.

Heiko Dachi: Parallel Stance. Inside of feet on line, with outside of feet in line with the outside of the hips or shoulders. Feet face forward and are parallel.

Hachiji Dachi *aka* **Shishen Kai:** Named this because the feet are in the shape of the kanji for the number eight *aka* Natural Stance. Feet are 45°, otherwise as in heiko dachi.

Uchi Hachiji Dachi *aka* **Kiba Dachi** *aka* **Nai Pan Dachi:** Inside Natural Stance. Feet face front by moving heels out, otherwise as in hachiji dachi.

Shiko Dachi: Straddle Leg Stance. The knees are pulled back. The soles of the feet grip the floor and the hips role forward. The hips are above the knees, back straight, chin in, shoulders relaxed and knees go straight into the ground. From heiko dachi, move toes out, move heel out and then move the toes out. This should be approximately double shoulder width apart. The toes are slightly visible. This is used to strengthen legs and for throws. Also used for dropping into techniques.

Sanchin Dachi: Three Battles Stance *aka* Hourglass Stance. The whole soles of the feet are stuck to the floor. Focus on the ankles, rotate the knees in and thighs out, pull the buttocks in and up.

Han Zenkutsu Dachi: Half Front Leaning Stance. There is one foot distance between feet. Back leg is straight but flexed. Front leg is turned slightly in, the back foot is close to straight. When blocking, the weight is evenly distributed. When punching, more weight is on the front leg. The width depends on the person but is usually hip or shoulder distance.

Zenkutsu Dachi: Front Leaning Stance. This is same as han zenkutsu dachi but with two feet distance forward.

Stances

Hikui Zenkutsu Dachi: Low Front Leaning Stance. It is similar to zenkutsu dachi only with three feet distance forward.

Kokutsu Dachi: Back Stance. This is similar to hikui zenkutsu dachi only turned sideways. Most of the weight is on the back bent leg and the toes are pointed 45°. Can be used for kicks.

Neko Ashi Dachi: Cat Stance. It is similar to a cat if you think of your back leg as the cat's back legs and your front leg as the cat's front legs. The similarity becomes apparent as you watch a cat play with a mouse. The front legs are light and the back legs are ready to pounce.

Back foot is 45°, front foot is one foot distance forward from the heel of the back foot. Back leg is bent. The front foot rests lightly on the ball of the foot and the front leg is slightly in. Hips are low, back is straight, chin is in, eyes are forward.

Bensoku Dachi: Cross Leg Stance, as in Seipai kata. The name means a small vine wrapping around a tree. The weight is even or more on back foot if necessary. Can be used for kicking.

Sesan Dachi: Side Facing Straddle Stance, as in Sesan Kata. One foot faces the front. The other faces the side. Otherwise the same as shiko dachi. Weight is 50/50.

Koshi Dachi: Squat Stance, as in Kururunfa Kata. This is the same as musubi dachi only with legs very bent. Used for throws. The heels come off the ground and apart when knees bend.

Renoji Dachi: Translation is the check "√" shape. Front foot is one-foot distance from the heel of the back foot. The position of the feet makes an "√" shape. Used for moving 45° towards an opponent. This is found in Seiyunchin Kata.

Sagiashi Dachi: Crane Leg Stance. Balance is maintained on one leg.

Stances

Moving in Stances

Sanchin: Begin in musubi dachi and move forward in a circular manner. The heels of the feet do not come off the ground. Move slowly and smoothly. Tighten after each step. Turn the leading heel in before stepping.

Neko Ashi Dachi: Basic- step forward with heel and draw rear leg up, Advanced- slide with soles of the feet on the floor. This can be done in all directions.

Zenkutsu Dachi: Step straight through when striking or with other linear techniques. Use circular movements while blocking. This will keep the head and hips level. Move the front heel in before moving.

Shiko Dachi: Basic- circular movement. Advanced- straight step.

Tai Sabaki and Suri Ashi

Tai Sabaki *aka* **Tai Hiraki:** Body shifting. Always uses hips.

Suri Ashi: Foot sliding.

Tai Sabaki Drill 1: Stay in heiko dachi and twist the body as if to avoid a punch.

Tai Sabaki Drill 2: Slide forward and back at a 45° angles beginning with heiko dachi and progressing through other stances.

Tai Sabaki Drill 3: Slide side-to-side, beginning with heiko dachi and progressing through other stances.

Tai Sabaki Drill 4: Moving in all directions with a natural stance. The body is free of tension. Feet are constantly in touch with the floor but not rooted. Always use the hips.

Suri Ashi Drill 1: Moving forward as in Sesan Kata. The feet face directly forward without tension. Snap the heel up to the buttocks and move forward. Can be done in all directions.

Stances

Tai Sabaki with a Partner

Moving with sabaki should be done with only the minimum necessary movement to avoid the attack and deliver the counter. Using slight shifts forward allows the whole body strength to be used effectively. Learning to judge distance is one benefit of sabaki training.

Tai Sabaki Partner Drill 1:
Tori attacks hidari mae geri.
Uke blocks with hidari hiza soto uke, then sabakis forward and kicks gedan hidari mae geri.

Tai Sabaki Partner Drill 2:
Tori attacks mae geri.
Uke uses hips and moves to side (evades). He immediately counters with mawashi geri, setting foot down in front.

Tai Sabaki Partner Drill 3:
Tori attacks mae geri.
Uke moves hips forward towards the kick to evade, then delivers gedan mawashi geri to supporting leg.

Tai Sabaki Partner Drill 4:
Tori attacks mae geri (left and right repeatedly).
Uke does sabaki to evade. Sabaki is done in all directions. Remember: eyes forward, chin in and down, shoulders free of tension, use the hips, flex the joints of the legs, slide lightly on the floor. Always sabaki just enough to be in the best position to counter. Slipping techniques can be done if contact is made.

Upper Body Sabaki Drills

1. Squat to avoid mikazuki geri. Be in good position to counter.

2. Use the focus pads to jab and sweep as uke bobs and weaves.

Blocking Techniques

Introduction

Almost all blocks can be done morote (double). Almost all can also be done open and closed handed. Please remember that blocks are practiced using big movements. This is to develop power and flexibility. Later, during kumite, these blocks can be made smaller and more focused. Each block must also be thought of as a strike as well. Powerful blocks can hurt and break.

Closed Hand Blocks

Jodan Age Uke: High Level Rising Block. Take the shortest distance from chamber to chin, then turn the forearm as the block finishes. End with the block one fist distance away from the head

Chudan Yoko Uke: Middle Level Block. Begin with hand in chamber coming across the body, then out, then out in a circular motion finishing by pulling the arm back to the side. Fist ends at shoulder level, wrist straight, power focused on the outside of the forearm.

Gedan Harai Uke: Low Level Abdomen Block. This block is very effective as a strike. From chamber, bring across the face, down across the body, finishing one fist distance above the leg.

Jodan Soto Uke: High Outside Block. This block begins from chamber but moves slightly inside, up and to the outside. It ends in the position as if you had just moved it straight up out of chamber. The elbow is slightly higher than the shoulder.

Chudan Uchi Uke: Middle Level Forearm Block. Start from chamber and bring the arm up, then across the body toward the inside. The wrist should end at the far side of the body. Turn the forearm as you finish the block.

Gedan Uchi Uke: Low Level Striking Block. This is done much like gedan hara uke but to the inside. This can be done open handed.

Juji Uke: "X" Block. This block can be done open or closed handed, high and to the side (for protection against mawashi geri). This can also be done low to protect against a kick.

Blocking Techniques

Tettsui Otoshi Uke: Hammer Fist Downward Block. This is very powerful and used to attack the weapon, meaning opponent's arm or leg.

Hiji Uke *aka* **Kuri Uke:** Elbow Block. This is very good for people who are not generally strong. This can be done by slipping the punch to the side, hitting them to the inside (naname) and up. These blocks work well against attacks to the side and back.

Open Hand Blocks

Jodan Haishu Age Uke: High Level Back Hand Rising Block as in Sesan Kata. The back of the hand, wrist and forearm are used to block with. From the chudan position, the hand moves forward and straight up to block. Keep the elbow down.

Shotei Yoko Uke: Palm Heel Inside Block. Keep the palm tight and thumb in. This is good for striking the elbow while blocking.

Mawashi Uke: Turning Block. The hand is placed face down under the elbow of the opposite hand. With muchimi, the hands move as if turning a wheel. Focus on the outsides of the hands to press and turn.

Jodan Haishu Nagashi Uke: High Deflecting Block. People with less strength need to block sooner and deflect the punch away. This block draws the opponent's strength in and deflects it at a 45° angle to the outside. The body must move with the block to be effective.

Jodan Morote Yoko Uke: High Double Side Block *aka* Praying Mantis Block. Wrists stay relaxed during this block.

Yoko Ko Uke: Side Bent Wrist Block. Begin at the solar plexus and block out.

Jodan Age Ko Uke: High Level Rising Bent Wrist Block. Begin at the solar plexus and block up.

Hiki Uke: Open Hand Gripping and Pulling Block. This can be done jodan as well.

Blocking Techniques

Chudan Morote Hiki Uke: Middle Level Double Open Hand Gripping and Pulling Block. This sets up a control for the opponent's arm.

Hiashu Otoshi Uke: Back Hand Downward Block. This is a block with back of hand, wrist and forearm. The hand begins at solar plexus and does a circular motion as it blocks down.

Shotei Otoshi Uke: Palm Heel Downward Block. Practice this much like beating two drums, one under each hand. This can also be done to the inside at chudan level.

Sukui Uke: Scooping Block, as in Saifa Kata. Hit the elbow and always cover with the free hand

Juji Uke: "X" Block. This can be done as explained before but to the side and open handed to protect against a mawashi geri as a set up for a throw.

Kaisho Gedan Barai: Open Hand Downward Block. It is the same as gedan barai but with open hands. It sets up for a grab.

Hiashu Juji Uke: "X" Block With Back Of Hand. This can be done against a kick. This works very well against a weapon attack and sets up for a throw.

Morote Gedan Shotei Uke: Double Palm Heel Low Level Block. The palms cross as in yoi position. This block can be used at chudan level and as a push.

Knee and Shoulder Blocks

Age Hiza Uke: Rising Knee Block. The knee rises as high as the elbow to form a "wall". Can be used against a mawashi geri.

Hiza Soto Uke: Knee Block To Outside. The knee makes a motion similar to mikazuki geri. This can be used against a mae geri.

Hi Soto Uke: High Foot Block. Block with foot both inside and out. It is similar to mikazuki geri.

Shoulder Block: No translation needed. The shoulders and hips are used to block the attack.

Punching Techniques

Introduction

Punching techniques can be divided into zuki (straight) and uchi (any other direction). The body should be relaxed until the last second and then you should tighten, focus and release. Hip movements are vital as in all areas of kihon.

How to Make a Fist

First make a bear claw with the fingers. Then roll all of the fingers down and cross the thumb over the index and middle fingers.

The most basic chamber is with the fist in the middle space between the armpit and the hip; usually next to the last full rib. As the punch leaves the body, the fist starts to rotate. Just as it nears ¾ completion, squeeze hard and finish the rotation. Ten pennies can be used to make sure each fist stays tight during drill. One penny is between each finger and the palm. Another is between the thumb and the fist.

Punching Techniques

Seiken Choku Zuki: Straight First Two Knuckle Punch. This is done to the eye for jodan, ganka for chudan and bladder for gedan.

Tate Zuki: Standing Fist Punch. This begins the same way as seiken zuki but is vertical when completed. This can be done high, middle and low.

Ura Zuki: Forward Punch. The back of the fist faces the floor. It goes straight out with the fist ending slightly higher than the elbow.

Age Zuki: Rising Punch. This is the same as ura zuki but is used for jodan. The target is the chin.

Mawashi Zuki: Turning Punch *aka* Roundhouse Punch. Chamber is the same as seiken zuki. Make a circular motion from side to jodan level.

Furi Zuki: Circular Swinging Punch. Fist comes from behind back.

Tettsui Uchi: Hammer Fist Strike as in Saifa Kata. This can also be done to the front in a variety of ways: inside, outside, diagonally (*naname*).

Punching Techniques

Uraken Uchi: Snapping Back Fist. This can be done forward and to the side.

Ura Uchi (not zuki)**:** Back Fist Strike. Use all of the back of fist, as in Saifa Kata.

Ude Uchi: Forearm Strike. Use all of back of fist and forearm. These can be done jodan, chudan, and gedan to the side and back. They can also be done to the front by naname (diagonally).

Kagi Zuki: Crossing Punch. Used to strike an opponent's ribs. Power comes from the twisting motion.

Yama Zuki: Mountain Punch. This is much like throwing a ball. Seiken are the focus.

Open Hand Techniques

Shuto Uchi *aka* **Sto Uchi:** Knife Hand Strike. This can be done jodan, chudan, gedan, naname and otoshi.

Haito Uchi: Ridge Hand Strike. The strike is done with the meaty part of hand between thumb and index finger. This is often used for a strike to throat.

Nukite: Finger Strike. The strike often comes from below and up.

Nihon Nukite: Two-Finger Strike. Index and middle finger used to strike.

Shotei Zuki: Palm Heel Strike. This can be done at a variety of levels

Ko Uchi: Back of Wrist Strike. This can be done to the side and front.

Yubi Hasami: Finger Pinch. This is used to grab and strike the forearm, ears, eyes, groin and throat. This is the proverbial "Kung Fu" grip.

Elbow Strikes

Hiji Ate *aka* **Empi uchi:** Elbow Strike. The underside of elbow is used to strike down or to the rear. Front of the elbow used to strike forward.

Punching Techniques

Jodan Yoko Hiji Ate: High Side Elbow Strike. The twisting motion of the body increases power to the strike. Strike comes from normal chamber to inside (temple).

Yoko Hiji Ate: Side Elbow Strike. This is done to chudan (outside).

Styles of Punches

Jun Zuki: One-Inch Punch. Full power is done in a short distance.

Oi Zuki: Lunge Punch. The punching hand is over the forward leg.

Gyaku Zuki: Reverse Punch. This is a strong punch with the opposite arm of the forward leg.

Kizami: Jab *aka* Leading Punch. This is a fast strike and often stuns an opponent.

Fist Formation

Keikoken: Knuckle Fist. The thumb is behind or inside of bent index finger.

Haito: Ridge Hand Fist. This uses the meaty part of hand between index finger and thumb.

Shotei: Palm Heel Fist. Keep the palm white and tight. Thumbs stay in.

Nakadaka Ipponken: Middle Finger Knuckle Fist. This is used in Seipai Kata.

Boshi Ken: Thumb Fist. Straighten the thumb and push down on the fist.

Heikoken *aka* **Hiraken** *aka* **Keiken:** Raking Fist. This is same as normal fist but with thumb on the side. The area between the middle joints of the fingers and the last joint of the fingers are the contact areas. Used for raking strikes like a cat. This is very powerful to the ears.

Punching Techniques

Double Hand Techniques

Almost all techniques can be done this way but without the retraction of the other hand, power can be lost.

Awase Zuki: "U" Punch as in Gekisai Dai Ichi Kata. The bottom hand is over the forward leg.

Hasami Zuki: Scissors Punch. Both hands punch inward trapping the opponent between them.

Kicking Techniques

Introduction

The legs are the body's strongest part. They can be used to end a fight outright. Because of this, some styles will focus 70% of their training on legs and 30% on hands. In Goju, we focus on each equally. One drawback to kicking is it uses up more energy, thus requiring more stamina.

When practicing, kicks should be evenly divided between air kicks and focus shield kicks. Air kicks develop form. Focus shield kicks develop power and stamina.

Low kicks are as effective as high kicks. "Cut down a tree by starting at the base," is a common analogy for the benefits of a good strong low kick. The shin, toes, ball of foot, outside of the foot, inside of the foot and the top of the foot can be used to attack with.

There are three main categories of performing kicks: kekomi, keage, and tobi geri. Most kicks can be done in all three categories as well as jodan (high), chudan (middle) and gedan (low).

The first category is kekomi. This is a thrust kick where the hip is used to drive the kick forward. This type of kick is good for stopping an opponent's drive, turning an opponent, and breaking. This is a powerful way to deliver a kick.

The second category is keage. This is a snapping kick, which prevents the opponent from catching the kick, and is used to do continuous combinations in a forward motion. Most of the kicks in Goju Ryu kata are of this category. Concentrate on the front leg muscles when extending and the back leg muscles when retracting.

The third category is tobi geri. This is a jumping kick. To do this, jump forward and up (as if stepping on a table) and kick with the back leg. These kicks should be delivered in a forward motion and not up. This is especially useful with hiza geri. Tobi geri is found in Suparinpei Kata and in one version of Sanseru Kata.

Kicking Techniques

Kicks

Sokuto Geri: Foot Sole Kick. This can be used for sweeping.

Sokuto Fumikomi Geri: Foot Sole Stomping Kick. In heiko dachi, sweep and stomp the opponent's foot. This can be done toward yourself from the front as well as the side.

Gedan Geri: Low Kick. Focus attention on the ball of the foot as you strike.

Kakato Ushiro Geri: Heel Back Kick, as in Sesan Kata. Try to kick your backside with your heel. This is done in two ways: bringing the heel directly up; and sweeping as if throwing sand backward. This can be used as a groin kick in a scooping fashion.

Mae Geri: Front Kick. From heiko dachi bring the leg up high and use the hip thrust as you snap the leg forward. This can be delivered at low , middle and high levels using kekomi, keage and tobi geri. Any part of the leg from the knee to the heel can be used. It is suggested people start with the front of the foot.

Kin Geri: Groin Kick. This is the same as mea geri but it is aimed at the groin. Use the hips and snap the knee to aim the kick at groin level.

Mawashi Geri: Turning Kick _aka_ Roundhouse Kick. There are many types of mawashi geri. In actual combat it is best to use the type most suited for the individual's body type.

This kick can be delivered in a circular motion down, evenly to the side, and in a circular upward motion. Basic mawashi geri starts with a large circular motion. From heiko dachi (possibly musubi dachi), pivot the supporting foot and follow with the hips as the leg travels in a circular motion to strike. The leg should be free of tension. The ball of the foot, the heel, the shin and occasionally the top of the foot can be used to strike with. This writer warns that the top of the foot has little protection and care must be given when using it.

Kicking Techniques

Kakato Fumikomi Geri: Heel Stomp Kick. The leg comes up and crosses at an angle to the inside, placing the body weight into the kick.

Ushiro Geri: Back Kick. Lift leg high in front then kick back. Keep the body arched as the kick is delivered. Kime by tightening the back, buttocks, and rear leg muscles. Look as you deliver the kick. After the basic movement has been accomplished successfully, fire the kick off from the ground without brining it forward.

Kakato Otoshi Geri: Heel Dropping Kick. The leg swings slightly in (or out), up and down, focusing on the heel. Land on the ball of the foot to prevent injuries.

Yoko Geri *aka* **Sokuto Yoko Geri** *aka* **Kansetsu Geri** *aka* **Gedan Sokuto Geri:** Low Level Foot Edge Kick. This is very effective against the knee joint. Lift the knee high and kick 45°. This kick is done this way in kata but is equally effective to the side. This kick works well against an opponent's side, front and back. This is also a good raking kick to the shin.

Sokuto Furi Geri: Sole of Foot Circular Kick, as in Suparinpei Kata. The leg swings up from the outside. The foot sole makes contact with the oposite hand, then returns. It is used against the leg, arm or head of an opponent. This is very good to practice on the heavy bag or focus shield.

Hiza Geri: Knee Kick. Pull the opponent to the knee as it is brought up.

Kaiten Ushiro Mawashi Geri: Spinning Backward Turning Kick. The hips initiate the movements as the leg comes around. Focus on the heel.

Gyaku Mawashi Geri: Reverses Round Kick *aka* Inside Hook Kick. Kick from heiko dachi. Bring the foot up, kicking to the outside, using the ball of the foot. It is possible to use the opponent's leg as a guide when kicking to the groin.

Mikazuki Geri: Crescent Kick. This is similar to sokuto furi geri but the kick continues all the way from the starting position through to the floor. This can be done from the outside or from the inside.

Kihon Ni and San

Introduction

Kihon Ni is two techniques in a sequence. This can be expanded to incorporate every stance and possibly even two stances with the same or different techniques.

Kihon San is three techniques sometimes delivered in a variety of stances. If more were to be created, it would be wise to look at evasion, faking attaching and throwing. Kicks can be done at gedan, chudan and jodan level in series for kihon san.

Like other kihon, these can be done in a variety of stances. This is why stances are often not specified here.

Kihon Ni Drills

1. Yoko tettsui uchi (could be gedan, chudan or jodan) and gyaku zuki
2. Zenkutsu dachi, gyaku zuki shift into heiko dachi at 45° and kagi zuki
3. Otoshi hiji ate, gyaku zuki
4. Hiki uke, tate zuki
5. Mae geri, yama zuki
6. gedan zuki, hiza geri
7. Kansetsu geri (set foot down in front), gyaku zuki
8. Hiza geri, gedan zuki (gyaku zuki)
9. Mikazuki, gyaku zuki
10. Judan uke, jodan zuki
11. Yoko uke, chudan zuki
12. Gedan uke, gedan zuki
13. Judan ko uke, shuto uchi
14. Ude uke, uraken uchi
15. Hiza geri, otoshi hiji ate

The following can be done with the same limb or alternating limbs:
16. Two kicks, one count
17. Two blocks, one count
18. Two strikes, one count

Kihon San Drills

1. Gedan gyaku, tettsui zuki uchi with other hand
2. Three strikes, same hand
3. Three strikes, alternating hands
4. Three blocks, alternating hands
5. Block jodan, chudan, gedan with the same hand
6. Block jodan, chudan, gedan alternating hands
7. Block gedan, chudan, jodan alternating hands
8. Block gedan, chudan, jodan same hand
9. Execute mawashi geri in a gedan, chudan, jodan sequence on one count, returning the foot to the ground each time (one count can be done with other kicks such as mae geri and yoko geri)
10. Jodan uke, ude uke, gyaku zuki

Kihon Ido

Introduction

Kihon ido can be practiced with a kiai after each technique. Turning has been done differently by each group I have been with. The main thing to keep in mind is that you are turning into a technique, so you need to be ready! I prefer to just turn, block and stop. Several techniques can be put together as the students' skill level increases. Jiyu ido kihon is free style moving basics. Taking one kata and trying to do all the movements from that kata then several kata, and so on can practice it. Every technique can be practiced in just about every stance while moving. Be creative. Some things to focus on are listed here. Kihon ido can be done slowly for beginners. As students get more advanced, they should focus on distance, speed and power.

Kihon Ido Drills

1. Sanchin dachi, mawashi geri, ushiro geri
2. Han zenkutsu dachi, step forward and execute morote shotei zuki, morote tettsui uchi
3. Zenkutsu dachi, move 45°, shift to heiko dachi and execute morote hasami zuki
4. Zenkutsu dachi step forward and execute oi yoko shuto uchi (like Gekisai Kata), then gyaku shuto zuki, then hiza geri (if you set the foot down in front then you alternate sides)
5. Sanchin dachi stepping forward, nihon oi tettsui uchi, gyaku zuki
6. Han zenkutsu dachi shifting forward, smash face as in Saifa Kata (fist into palm), gedan hara uke, gyaku zuki
7. Sanchin dachi, jodan uke, seiken zuki
8. Zenkutsu dachi, gyaku zuki, oi zuki
9. Shiko dachi 90°, seiken zuki
10. Shiko dachi, gedan harai uke, gyaku zuki
11. Han zenkutsu dachi, mae geri, mawashi geri
12. Zenkutsu dachi, mae geri, oi zuki
13. Zenkutsu dachi, mae geri, hiji ate, uraken uchi, gedan uke, gedan gyaku zuki (as in Gekisai Kata)
14. Shiko dachi, age zuki, uraken uchi, gedan uke, gyaku seiken zuki (similar to Seiyunchin Kata)

Neko Ashi Kihon

Introduction

Neko ashi dachi is one of the quintessential Goju Ryu stances. Neko ashi dachi takes a lot of practice. In times past, it may not have been as low as we practice it today but it is always good to push yourself to stay low.

Neko Ashi Ido

Neko ashi ido can be practiced while holding a focus shield on your head. This reinforces good posture. Good posture enables a person to move quickly and accurately. The front foot steps forward and the heel is placed on the ground. The hips pull the back foot up quickly as the front foot changes to the ball of the foot. The distance of the front foot is one to one and one half "foot" distance from the back.

Neko Ashi Ido Drills

From neko ashi dachi, slide forward and execute the following:
(Unless otherwise specified)
1. Neko ashi dachi, step into han zenkutsu dachi, strike oi zuki, mawashi geri off back leg setting foot down in front, strike oi zuki, return to neko ashi dachi and repeat
2. Neko ashi dachi, mikazuki geri, oi zuki, gyaku zuki
3. Neko ashi dachi, ko uke (zuki) jodan, ura zuki
4. Neko ashi dachi, shift into shiko dachi and execute age zuki, then ura zuki
5. Neko ashi dachi, shift into zenkutsu dachi, oi hiji ate toward center from outside, uraken uchi with same hand
6. Mae geri with the front leg followed by kizami zuki and gyaku zuki.
7. Uchi uke and gyaku zuki
8. Joge uke (chudan/gedan block simultaneously, gedan block over front leg), mae geri and nihon zuki
9. Tora guchi (gedan hand over front leg), mawashi hiji ate (with the gedan hand), gyaku zuki
10. Jodan uke in sanchin dachi, gyaku zuki, and return to neko ashi dachi
11. Chudan yoko uke in zenkutsu dachi, gyaku zuki, return to neko ashi dachi
12. Gedan harai uke in shiko dachi, gyaku zuki, return to neko ashi dachi
13. Morote uchi uke (breaking opponent's arm), mae geri, and yoko tettsui uchi strike to opponent's head
14. Furi uchi and yoko uke (as in Seipai Kata), yoko geri, and oi tettsui uchi

Neko Ashi Kihon

Shippon Ido

Shippon ido means four directional movements. It is movement done to the positions on the clock. This is often done in neko ashi dachi but can be done in other stances as well.

1. In heiko dachi, face 12 o' clock
2. Step into hidari neko ashi dachi and execute hidari hiki uke
3. Turn to 6 o' clock in migi neko ashi dachi and execute migi hiki uke
4. Turn to 3 o' clock in hidari neko ashi dachi and execute hidari hiki uke
5. Turn to 9 o' clock in migi neko ashi dachi and execute migi hiki uke
6. Turn to 6 o' clock in hidari neko ashi dachi and execute hidari hiki uke
7. Turn to 12 o' clock in migi neko ashi dachi and execute migi hiki uke

Be creative. Use the same sequence as above but with sanchin dachi and jodan uke, or shiko dachi and gedan barai.

Top Ten Kihon List

This top ten list is a distilment of many techniques in Goju Ryu. It is a quick and dirty list that is by no means perfect. What this list tries to do is reduce some redundancy in the curriculum by looking at techniques as not just a block or a strike but a block *and* a strike. Nukite is not on the list of punches because hiki uke is on the list of blocks. This is because hiki uke can be considered a strike to the eyes as well as a block. This train of thought is followed throughout the list. Students can expect to be drilled heavily from this list during examinations.

Top Ten Strikes

1. Seiken Zuki
2. Age Zuki
3. Tettsui Zuki
4. Shotei Zuki
5. Ko Uke
6. Hiji Ate
7. Awase Zuki
8. Kagi Zuki
9. Shuto and Heito Uchi
10. Ura Zuki

Top Ten Kicks

1. Mae Geri
2. Ushiro Geri
3. Mawashi Geri
4. Gyaku Mawashi Geri
5. Yoko Geri
6. Kansetsu geri
7. Hiza geri
8. Mika Zuki Geri
9. Fume Komi Geri
10. Otoshi Geri

Top Ten Blocks

1. Jodan
2. Chudan
3. Gedan
4. Uchi Uke
5. Uchi Uke Gedan
6. Hiki Uke
7. Kosa Uke
8. Osae Uke
9. Nagashi Uke
10. Sukui Uke

Top Ten Stances

1. Heiko Dachi
2. Sanchin Dachi
3. Zenkutsu Dachi
4. Shiko Dachi
5. Neko Ashi Dachi
6. Hachiji Dachi
7. Sagiashi Dachi
8. Kosa Dachi
9. Heisoku Dachi
10. Musubi Dachi

Kihon

Notes

_____

_____

_____

_____

_____

_____

_____

_____

_____

_____

_____

_____

_____

_____

_____

_____

_____

_____

_____

_____

_____

_____

_____

_____

_____

_____

_____

_____

_____

_____

_____

_____

Chapter 5

Renzoku and Taikyoku

Chapter 5 Table of Contents

Renzoku Introduction

Renzoku Ichi-Ju (combinations 1-10) were developed by Sensei Steve Wilson. It was his intent to bridge a gap between kihon and kata. They focus on generating perfect form and power. Some are used to develop fluidity as well. All can be done on both sides, with partners as yakusoku kumite, on focus shields and as renzoku ido. One of my favorite ways to do Renzoku is doing the same renzoku on both the migi and hidari side in one count. Many renzoku may be done in a linear fashion. Done in this way, each side will often alternate and be a good overall kihon ido. Another way to do Renzoku is to do Renzoku Dai Ichi on one side and Dai Ni on the other. Then do Renzoku Dai San on the first side. Continue this pattern through Renzoku Dai Ju.

Renzoku ido is something new introduced here in this manual, as is something that is jokingly named, "Renzoku Dai Mike." Renzoku Dai Mike is my own creation. I feel that at least trying to develop your own renzoku is a valuable way of understanding all renzoku better. My renzoku is not meant to be an example of "Divine Revelation," only as an illustration of a tool in my own research. I hope people will enjoy it and learn form it.

Beginning Renzoku

Renzoku Dai Ichi

From heiko dachi no kamae, step back into hidari sanchin dachi and block hidari jodan uke. Kick migi mae geri to groin, setting foot down forward into migi han zenkutsu dachi. Execute migi jodan zuki with kiai. Execute hidari and migi chudan. Step back into hidari sanchin dachi and execute hidari jodan uke. Return to heiko dachi no kamae.

Renzoku Dai Ni

From heiko dachi no kamae, step back into hidari zenkutsu dachi and execute hidari chudan yoko uke. Kick migi mae geri to the groin, setting foot down in migi zenkutsu dachi. Execute migi tate zuki to solar plexus with kiai. Execute hidari and migi chudan zuki. Step back hidari zenkutsu dachi and execute hidari chudan yoko uke. Return to heiko dachi no kamae.

Renzoku Dai San

From heiko dachi no kamae, step back into hidarai shiko dachi and execute hidari gedan hari uke. Execute a migi mawashi geri to opponent's ribs, setting foot down into migi shiko dachi. Immediately execute a migi hiji ate to opponents rib cage with kiai. Then, execute hidari and migi chudan zuki. Pivot back into hidari shiko dachi and execute hidari gedan harai uke. Resume heiko dachi no kamae.

Renzoku Dai Yon

From heiko dachi no kamae, step back into hidari sanchin dachi and execute hidari hiki uke. Kick right mae geri gedan, setting foot down in migi han zenkutsu dachi. Immediately execute right tettsui uchi to clavicle with kiai. Execute hidari and migi chudan zuki. Step back into hidari sanchin dachi and execute hidarai hiki uke. Resume heiko dachi no kamae.

Intermediate Renzoku

Renzoku Dai Go

From heiko dachi no kamae, step back into hidarai sanchin dachi and execute hidari jodan uke, followed by migi chudan yoko uke, followed by hidarai gedan barai. Execute chudan migi mae geri, setting foot down in migi shiko dachi at a 45° angle. Execute migi age zuki (with kiai), otoshi hiji ate, hiji ate, uraken uchi, gedan barai. Execute hidari and migi chudan zuki. Pivot the migi leg back into hidari shiko dachi and execute left gedan harai uke. Return to heiko dachi no kamae.

Renzoku Dai Roku

From heiko dachi no kamae, step back into left neko ashi dachi. Execute left jodan ko uke and kick chudan migi mae geri, setting foot down in migi han zenkutsu dachi. Immediately execute migi shuto uchi (with kiai) while covering forehead with hidari teisho uke. Execute hidari yoko tettsui uchi jodan. Execute migi jodan zuki followed by left chudan zuki. Step back with migi leg into hidari neko ashi dachi and execute hidari jodan ko uke. Return to heiko dachi no kamae.

Renzoku Dai Shichi

From heiko dachi no kamae (with hands up in jodan kumite kamae), sabaki back to the counterclockwise at 45° while executing hidarai shotei jodan uke. Sabaki back clockwise while executing a migi jodan shotei uke. Kick migi mae geri gedan, setting foot down in front and execute migi oi zuki, migi mawashi hiji ate, migi yoko hiji ate and hidari hiza geri with kiai. Return to heiko dachi no kamae.

Advanced Renzoku

Renzoku Dai Hachi

From heiko dachi no kamae, pivot counterclockwise (using tai sabaki) and block morote hiki uke. Execute migi mae geri chudan, set the foot down in front and execute migi ude uchi jodan while pivoting the body 90° counterclockwise (envision having clothes lined an attacker, turned him and thrown him to the ground), bend forward and execute hidarai seiken zuki, migi seiken zuki, followed by migi kakato geri gedan (the kick may be substituted with fumi kekomi geri or kansetsu geri gedan). Return to heiko dachi no kamae.

Renzoku Dai Ku

From hidarai neko ashi no kamae, execute hidarai mae geri to groin area. Pivot and execute a migi ushiro geri to the front. Set the foot down in migi han zenkutsu dachi and execute a migi uraken uchi to nose level followed by a gyaku zuki. Slide right foot back slightly into migi neko ashi with hands in chudan no kamae, and execute migi mae geri. Slide foot back into hidarai neko ashi dachi and execute hidarai mawashi geri jodan. Return to heiko dachi no kamae.

Renzoku Dai Ju

From heiko dachi no kamae, tai sabaki to the clockwise 45° quickly and powerfully, as if to avoid a kick. At the same time, execute hidarai mae geri and set the foot down in front. Follow with oi zuki, gyaku zuki, then migi mawashi geri jodan. Return to heiko dachi no kamae.

Renzoku Dai Mike

From hidarai neko ashi dachi no kamae, mae geri off the front leg. Execute hidarai shotei zuki. Grab the hair and pull the opponent down to ground. Execute kakato geri to the back of the opponent's neck. Return to heiko dachi no kamae.

Renzoku Ido

These Renzoku Ido focus on some of the key techniques of each renzoku.

1. Sanchin dachi, mae geri, jodan zuki

2. Zenkutsu dachi, mae geri, tate zuki

3. Shiko dachi, mawashi geri, mawashi hiji ate

4. Zenkutsu dachi, migi mae geri, tettsui uke

5. Shiko dachi mawashi geri, age zuki jodan, otoshi hiji ate, mae hiji ate, uraken uchi, gedan hara uke, gyaku zuki, repeat

6. Hidarai neko ashi dachi, slide forward, execute hidarai jodan ko uke, kick off back leg mae geri setting foot down in front into han zenkutsu dachi, execute right shuto uchi while covering forehead with hidarai teisho uke, execute hidarai yoko tettsui uchi to temple, slide foot back to migi neko dachi, repeat

7. Sabaki backward into heiko dachi at 45°, execute jodan shotei uke, mae geri off back leg, set foot down in back, repeat by switching sides

8. Tai sabaki forward at 45°, execute morote hiki uke, mae geri off back leg, setting foot down in front, repeat

9. From hidarai neko ashi dachi, mae geri of front leg, pivot and ushiro geri to front, setting foot down in migi han zenkutsu dachi and execute a migi ura ken uchi to nose level, followed by gyaku zuki, slide foot back into migi neko ashi in chudan no kamae, repeat

10. From heiko dachi, tai sabaki back to the right as if to avoid a kick, execute hidarai mae geri, oi zuki, followed by gyaku zuki, repeat by doing tai sabaki the other way

Note: Many renzoku may be done in a linear fashion. Done in this way, each side will often alternate and be a good overall kihon ido.

Taikyoku

Taikyoku Introduction

There is wide interpretation on the meaning of the name Taikyoku. It has been said to mean, "wide view", "see clearly", 'first cause', and "first course". Certainly, the general consensus is that Taikyoku means something that is learned early and is comprehensive.

Giyo Yoshitaka Funakoshi (the son of Gichin Funikoshi, the founder of Shotokan Karate) developed the Taikyoku pattern. It is an "H" pattern which is done with a series of turns. Some of the turns are 90°, others are 180° and 270°. He named his three original Taikyoku Shodan, Taikyoku Nidan and Taikyoku Sandan.

Later the Goju Kai founder Gogen Yamaguchi took the "H" pattern and expanded it into a set of five . Each set has an ichi and ni component for a total of ten. The ten Taikyoku are Taikyoku Jodan Ichi and Ni, Taikyoku Chudan Ichi and Ni, Taikyoku Gedan Ichi and Ni, Taikyoku Kake Uke Ichi and Ni and Taikyoku Mawashi Uke Ichi and Ni.

Some organizations only practice a few of the Taikyoku such as Jodan Ni, Chudan Ni and Gedan Ni because they feel the Taikyoku are redundant. Many organizations also refer to the Taikyoku as "waza" (movement) as opposed to kata because they have limited applications and were recently created.

Taikyoku Kanji

大局上段一
Taikyoku Jodan Ichi

大局上段二
Taikyoku Jodan Ni

大局中段一
Taikyoku Chudan Ichi

大局中段二
Taikyoku Chudan Ni

大局下段一
Taikyoku Gedan ichi

大局下段二
Taikyoku Gedan Ni

大局欠け受け一
Taikyoku Kake Uke Ichi

大局欠け受け二
Taikyoku Kake Uke Ni

大局回し受け一
Taikyoku Mawashi Uke Ichi

大局回し受け二
Taikyoku Mawashi Uke Ni

Taikyoku Descriptions

The typical Taikyoku pattern is described here using Taikyoku Chudan Ichi.

Taikyoku Kata Chudan Ichi

1. From yoi position, turn 90° into hidari zenkutsu dachi and block hidari gedan barai.

2. Step into migi zenkutsu dachi and punch oi zuki with kiai.

3. Turn 180° and block migi gedan barai in migi zenkutsu dachi.

4. Step into hidari zenkutsu dachi and punch oi zuki.

5. Turn 90° and block hidari gedan barai in hidari zenkutsu dachi.

6. Step and punch oi zuki three times. Kiai on the third punch.

7. Turn 270° and block hidari gedan barai in hidari zenkutsu dachi.

8. Step and punch oi zuki.

9. Turn 180° and block migi gedan barai in migi zenkutsu dachi.

10. Step and punch oi zuki.

11. Turn 90° and block hidari gedan barai in hidari zenkutsu dachi.

12. Step and punch oi zuki three times. Kiai on the third punch.

13. Turn 270° and block hidari gedan barai in hidari zenkutsu dachi.

14. Step and punch oi zuki with kiai.

15. Return to yoi position using ibuki breathing (a deep, slow, deliberate breath)

Taikyoku Descriptions

These Taikyoku follow the same description as Taikyoku Chudan Ichi but with the insertion of the subsequent combinations of techniques.

Jodan Ichi
Sanchin Dachi-Jodan Uke
Sanchin Dachi-Oi Zuki

Jodan Ni
Sanchin dachi-Jodan Uke
Zenkutsu Dachi-Oi Zuki

Chudan Ichi
Zenkutsu Dachi-Chudan Yoko Uke
Zenkutsu Dachi-Oi Zuki

Chudan Ni
Sanchin Dachi-Chudan Yoko Uke
Zenkutsu Dachi-Oi Zuki

Gedan Ichi
Shiko Dachi-Gedan Barai
Shiko Dachi-Oi Zuki

Gedan Ni
Shiko Dachi-Gedan Barai
Zenkutsu Dachi-Oi Zuki

Kake Uke Ichi
Sanchin Dachi-Kake Uke
Sanchin Dachi- Hiji Ate
(with chamber hand in front of chest)

Kake Uke Ni
Sanchin Dachi-Kake Uke
(forward then back)
Sanchin Dachi-Mae Geri, Hiji Ate
(with chamber hand in front of chest)

Tora Guchi Ichi
Sanchin Dachi-Tora Guchi
Sanchin Dachi-Oi Zuki

Tora Guchi Ni
Sanchin Dachi-Tora Guchi,
Shiko Dachi-Oi Zuki

Renzoku and Taikyoku

Chapter 6

Kata and Bunkai

Chapter 6 Table of Contents

Kata and Bunkai

Introduction

Much has been written, video taped, and said about kata and bunkai. It is a sobering thought that we are doing kata and bunkai that people are doing across the globe and across the centuries. In one sense, it is a very large group experience to train kata and bunkai, yet in another sense, it is also a very personal one. I hope this information may help many others, yet if it helps only one, I will be satisfied.

Some of the elements to look for in kata include power, coordination, balance fluidity and flexibility. Movements need to have rhythm and elegance without being robotic. The practitioner needs to have a good focus and to look in the direction the technique is being performed. Proper body alignment and breathing that is in harmony with techniques are necessary.

It has been said, "The whole system is in one kata." So, look deeply. Originally, people may have only learned two or three kata. There was also no chronological order to which they were taught. Times have changed and most karate organizations teach all the kata in an order similar to what is presented here. I encourage people to learn all the kata then focus on two to four kata, working them feverishly!

Only the standard bunkai are presented. These are required for grading examinations. There are many other bunkai that can be researched and noted in the oyo bunkai section. Eventually, this oyo bunkai section will become larger and larger as the student becomes more advanced. Using oyo bunkai to break bones should be examined along with throws, eye strikes, chokes, and groin strikes. In days past, the bunkai often ended with a takedown, and almost always ended with a choke, eye gouge, or groin strike.

Some Goju Ryu organizations practice other kata that are not presented here. Meibukan Goju Ryu practice Tenshi, Seiryu, Byakko, Shujaku, and Genbu. The founder of Meibukan, Meitoku Yagi Sensei, developed these. The founder of Shorei Kan Goju Ryu, Seikichi Toguchi Sensei, developed Hokiyu Dai Ichi and Ni, Gekiha Dai Ichi and Ni, Kakuha Ichi and Ni, as well as Gakusei No Kata. In Goju Kai, Gogen Yamaguchi Sensei expanded the Taikyoku kata. Goju Kai also practices a combination of Sanchin and Tensho kata and Two White Crane Kata. The kata, which are presented here in this guidebook, are often found in many Goju Ryu curriculums.

Kata Names Study Guide

<u>**Heishugata**</u>
(Closed Kata)

<u>Sanchin</u>	<u>Three Battles</u>
<u>Tensho</u>	<u>Rotating Palms</u>

<u>**Kaishugata**</u>
(Open Kata)

<u>Gekisai Dai Ichi</u>	<u>Attack and Smash No. 1</u>
<u>Gekisai Dai Ni</u>	<u>Attack and Smash No. 2</u>
<u>Saifa</u>	<u>Smash and Tear</u>
<u>Seiyunchin</u>	<u>The Rule of Pulling in Battle</u>
<u>Shisochin</u>	<u>Four Directional Battle</u>
<u>Sanseiru</u>	<u>36 Hand Method</u>
<u>Seipai</u>	<u>18 Hand Method</u>
<u>Kururunfa</u>	<u>Long Stop At Once to Tearing</u>
<u>Sesan</u>	<u>13 Hand Method</u>
<u>Suparinpei</u>	<u>108 Hand Method</u>

Kata Kanji

三戦
Sanchin

転掌
Tensho

撃砕第一
Gekisai Dai Ichi

撃砕第二
Gekisai Dai Ni

砕破
Saifa

制引戦
Seiyunchin

四向戦
Shisochin

三十六手
Sanseiru

十八手
Seipai

久留頓破
Kururunfa

十三手
Sesan

壱百零八手
Suparinpei

手 This symbol is "Te" as in karate. It means " hand" and in a broader sense " method." This kanji is not pronounced but is left in to emphasize a strong Chinese background.

Often there is no standard reading of these kanji as compounds. There is some latitude in their interpretation. The translations of the Kata Names Study Guide are accurate but rudimentary. Students are encouraged to research further.

Additional Kata Information

Sanchin: This kata was originally the only kata that a student was taught for the first three years of practice. This kata along with hojo undo training was the basis for developing a karate body. Miyagi Chojun Sensei's version is a health kata which develops internal organs and strength. The turning version is more combative. The original open hand version develops nukite and is the most martial. I like to think of Sanchin, regardless of the version, as an energy gathering kata from three levels: jodan, chudan and gedan. They are metaphorical for Heaven, Body and Earth. They are also metaphorical for Body, Mind and Spirit. Although "chin" translates as "battle," the point of any battle is to win peace. In order to win battles, you need to gather energy; therefore, I like to think of Sanchin as a way to develop that energy.

Tensho: This kata was developed by Chojun Miyagi Sensei to emphasize the "Ju" aspects of Goju Ryu. It is considered his masterpiece. Its bunkai can be done working around an attacker. Miyagi Chojun Sensei developed this kata after studying Rokkishu Kata in China. He developed Tensho to compliment Sanchin Kata. This kata helps develop the "Ju" aspects of Goju Ryu.

Breathing can be developed in stages. The first stage emphasizes breathing directly into the tanden. The second stage emphasizes imagining the breath going up and in back of the head, down the back and in a circular motion into the tanden. The third stage emphasizes the breath going all the way to the feet. This is the same type of breathing as in Sanchin Kata.

Gekisai Dai Ichi and Ni: Chojun Miyagi Sensei and Sensei Shoshine Nagamine developed these kata in 1940. Some say these kata were to prepare students for war, others say to make a basic kata that would be quickly available to the general public. A mixture of these two explanations is probably closer to the truth. The emphasis in Gekisai Dai Ichi is on moving forward. Gekisai Dai Ni introduces open hand blocks, shifting (sabaki) and neko ashi dachi.

Gekisai Dai Ichi and Ni were introduced formally into the curriculum as a kata in 1948. It is important to remember that all techniques in all kata correspond to vital pints on a person of your same size, weight and gender. When executing techniques, keeping this in mind will help focus your concentration. It also helps to think that most vital points are the same size as an eyeball.

Additional Kata Information

Saifa: This is the first in the curriculum of a traditional Kaishugata (kaishu ~ *open*, the "o" in kaisho changes to a "u" and gata ~ *kata*, the "k" is changed to a "g" when it is preceded by another kanji). This kata really emphasizes moving to the side of an opponent. A good rule of thumb is that beginning kata teach straight on defense and attacks. Intermediate kata tend to teach defending and attacking from the side. Advanced kata teach getting behind an opponent.

Seiyunchin: It has been said that any kata with "chin" in the name can be thought of as energy gathering. There are at least two versions of this kata. They look very different as far as hand movements go but the stances are very similar. There are no kicks or sanchin dachi in this kata.

Shisochin: This kata can be done quickly or slowly. If it is done quickly, it develops striking. If it is done slowly, it is energy gathering. "Shi" translates as the number four. "Sho" translates as direction. "Chin," as in Sanchin and Seiyunchin, translates as battles. I like to think of this kata as gathering energy in four directions for much of the same reasons that I like to think of Sanchin as energy gathering. It has been said that this was one of Miyagi Chojun Sensei's favorite kata late in life. It is also well suited for tall people.

Sanseiru: I hope it is not sacrilegious to say that this may have been Miyagi Chojun Sensei's least favorite kata. Personally, if this is true, I believe it is because the kansetsu geri in the kata can damage the knee if it is not doneproperly. It is easy not to realize this until damage is done. So be careful not to hyper extend your leg. As with all Goju kata with numbers in the names, it has a strong Buddhist influence. This kata can also be done with tobi geri in the opening sequence.

Seipai: This kata involves various sliding movements. One sliding movement is done to get inside an opponent's defenses for pushing. This movement looks like a wave. It is unusual in its use of turns and angles. I believe it is to develop evasion, speed and balance.

Kururunfa: This kata is often taught at Yondan level although this varies among schools. This is thought to be Jinan Shinzato's best kata. He was Sensei Miyagi's top student prior to WWII.

Chapter 6: Kata and Bunkai

Additional Kata Information

*Sesan: This kata's name may have its origins in Buddhist concepts of numerology. Performing kata is often described as moving meditation. The Buddhists are known to have used "Mudra," or hand positions, to help with meditation. This kata, along with several other Goju Ryu kata, are said to have many of these mudra contained in them.

*Suparinpei: There are several ways to do this kata depending on the age and technical ability of the practitioner. The punches at the beginning can be done slowly as in sanchin dachi, or with muchimi. These ways are good for the older karateka. The punches can also be done full power. This is best for the younger karateka. This kata introduces a new type of breathing. This type of breathing is done in this format: breathe in before the technique, hold as the technique is executed and release after the kime.

*At the time of this writing, the author has only studied these kata through books and videos tapes. He has not had formal instruction on their performance.

Higaonna Morio Sensei (Traditional Okinawan Goju Ryu Karate-Do, Panther Production Video Tape, 1981) takes approximately the time listed below to perform each kata. These are benchmarks and individuals may vary slightly. The Heishugata are measured from yoi and the hands opening after the last yoi. The Kaishugata are measured from yoi to yoi.

Heishugata

Sanchin: 2 min. 15 sec.

Turning Sanchin: 1 min. 42 sec.

Tensho: 1 min. 42 sec.

Kaishugata

Gekisai Dai Ichi: 29 sec.

Gekisai Dai Ni: 35 sec.

Saifa: 35 sec.

Seiyunchin: 1 min. 40 sec.

Shisochin: 53 sec.

Sanseiru: 50 sec.

Seipai: 1 min. 11 sec.

Kururunfa: 1 min 10 sec.

Sesan: 1 min. 4 sec.

Suparinpei: 2 min 24 sec.

Kata Training Methods

1. Just hands technique
2. Just feet
3. Super slow
4. Super fast
5. Normal
6. Sanchin style
7. Sanchin style with partner performing light shime
8. Reverse
9. Flowing (Ju)
10. In street clothes
11. In the dark
12. Eyes closed
13. Different directions
14. Calling out each move
15. With weights
16. On different terrain
17. Linear (as a brain teaser)
18. Partners together
19. Partners opposite (one doing forward the other doing reverse)
20. Individually in front of a group
21. Do a squat after each technique
22. Remove the blocks (or punches)
23. Kick after every technique
24. Just offensive techniques
25. Doing each move ten times before going on
26. Turning version. For each sequence of two steps forward, replace the first step with a leg cross and a turn, ending as you would normally *aka* whirling dervish version.
27. Kiai on all punches, kicks or other attacks
28. Three techniques for each technique, alternate hands. This is good for reciprocating hip action.
29. Add an additional tobi geri before each kick
30. Combine several of the above e.g. Turning (#26), Kiai (#27), Tobi Geri (#29), or other combinations
31. Sabaki with every step.
32. Gekisai, or other kata, in only one stance such as shiko dachi or neko ashi dachi

A Typical Kata Curriculum

The following is the typical breakdown used by many Goju Ryu karate organizations of the order in which kata are taught. Originally, there was no order to the kata curriculum. Students began with Sanchin kata but would be assigned two or three kata to work on intensively depending on their knowledge, abilities, character and conduct. The original open hand version of Sanchin kata is presented in this guidebook after Seipai. It is not commonly known and therefore, it is an exception to the typical kata curriculum.

White Belt Kata and Bunkai

Sanchin

Gekisai Dai Ichi

Gekisai Dai Ni

Green Belt Kata and Bunkai

Turning Sanchin

Saifa

Seiyunchin

Brown Belt Kata and Bunkai

Tensho

Shisochin

Begin to Develop Oyo Bunkai

Black Belt Kata and Bunkai

These kata and bunkai are often taught at the ranks indicated.

Sanseru - Shodan

Seipai – Nidan

Kururunfa - Sandan

Sesan - Yondan

Suparinpei – Yondan/Godan

Continue to Develop Oyo Bunkai

The kata presented in this manual include Sanchin, Gekisai Dai Ichi, Gekisai Dai Ni, Turning Sanchin, Saifa, Seiyunchin, Tensho, Shisochin, Sanseru, Seipai and the Original Open hand Sanchin Kata. It is expected that students submit their own written explanation of the following kata and bunkai to the grading panel. These kata and bunkai include Kururunfa, Sesan and Suparinpei. This guidebook can be used as an example, a finger pointing at the moon if you will, to assist in this task.

Sanchin Kata

Sanchin Kata (Closed hand version developed by Miyagi Sensei):

1. Bow, then from yoi position, step into migi sanchin dachi and assume morote chudan yoko uke.
2. Breath in as you pull back hidari arm, and breathe out while striking with the same arm chudan zuki. Keep the other hand in chudan yoko uke position. Pull the punching hand back to chudan yoko uke position when finished
3. Step into hidari sanchin dachi. Breathe in as you pull back migi arm, and breathe out as you strike chudan zuki with the same hand, keeping the other hand in the chudan yoko uke position. Pull back the striking hand to chudan yoko uke when finished.
4. Step into migi sanchin dachi and repeat step 2.
5. Stay stationary and perform four chudan zuki, starting with migi and alternating hands. End in chudan morote yoko uke kamae.
6. Open hands. Rotate and press down forming a circle with the arms.
7. Grip with both hands, starting with the index fingers. Rotate the hands and pull back to chamber then strike out with nukite slowly.
8. Repeat step 7 for a total of three times.
9. Step backward into hidari sanchin dachi and execute tora guchi.
10. Step back into migi sanchin dachi and execute tora guchi.
11. Slide the right foot back into musubi dachi. Stand in yoi position and end by regulating breathing.
12. Return to yoi position and bow.

Sanchin Kata Special Considerations:

This section is rudimentary at best but important nonetheless. Sanchin is a very important kata.
1. All breathing is done slowly unless otherwise specified.
2. No breathing while stepping.
3. Keep heel on the floor while stepping.
4. Fast last inhalation.
5. Keep the chin down eyes forward, shoulders down and back.
6. The back is straight and fists tight.
7. The soles of the feet stay in contact with the floor the whole time
8. While stepping backward, try feel where you are going with your back muscles.

Sanchin Bunkai: None specified here.

Sanchin Kata

Shime:

Shime helps students with muscle alignment, concentration and harmonizing the mind, body and spirit. Shime begins from the back at foot level. Try to insert a finger under the sole of the feet and try to move the heels. Check the knees and the tension in the buttocks. Check the focus in the tanden. Then check the back. When striking the shoulders, do not do so without warning. Draw the hand across the shoulders before striking. Striking the student stimulates the mind, body and spirit. If the legs are uneven in strength, the student may tip to one side. Only strike on the exhale. Shime is then done from the front, starting at the top. Check the student's punch by providing resistance to the chudan yoko uke and the punch at the same time. Kicking between the legs can assure the groin is protected. Tettsui uchi can be done on the thighs to check tension. Strikes to the stomach are done after the punch is extended. The thighs can be hit, kicked or slapped to check tension. This can be done from the back as well.

The following are guidelines for providing the intensity of shime to students.

White Belt:
Light, without movement.

Green Belts:
Medium, with movement.

Brown Belts:
Hard, with movement.
This is done with adult males only. All others stay at medium.

Black Belts:
Hard with more repetitions. Also, students must learn to give shime.

Gekisai Dai Ichi Kata

Gekisai Dai Ichi Kata:

1. Bow, then from yoi, pivot into hidarai sanchin dachi, jodan age uke.
2. Step into migi han zenkutsu dachi, oi zuki jodan.
3. Step back into shiko dachi and block hidarai gedan hara uke.
4. Step into migi sanchin dachi, jodan age uke.
5. Step into hidarai han zenkutsu dachi, hidarai oi zuki.
6. Step back into shiko dachi and block migi gedan hara uke.
7. Step into hidarai sanchin dachi, hidarai chudan yoko uke.
8. Step into migi sanchin dachi, migi chudan yoko uke.
9. Kick hidarai mae geri, age hiji ate, uraken uchi, gedan barai and gedan gyaku zuki. Kiai.
10. Sweep with back leg and shuto.
11. Step through into hidarai sanchin dachi, hidarai chudan yoko uke.
12. Kick migi mae geri, migi age hiji ate, uraken uchi, gedan barai, gedan gyaku zuki. Kiai.
13. Sweep with the back foot and shuto.
14. Pull back into migi zenkutsu dachi and strike morote zuki.
15. Step up and then back into hidarai zenkutsu dachi and strike awase zuki.
16. Step forward.
17. Return to the yoi position and bow.

Gekisai Dai Ichi Kata Special Considerations:

1. Low shiko dachi.
2. Keep back straight.
3. Use muchimi on chudan yoko uke's.
4. Have shoulders close together for shuto.
5. While executing jodan age uke, the elbow is pulled down slightly to deflect the power of the punch.
6. Step straight on the punches and pull the chamber hand back hard.
7. The soles of the feet grip the floor in shiko dachi. The shinbones are slightly in from perpendicular and the hips are rolled forward.
8. The gedan barai is one fist distance away from the knee.
9. Stomp down hard after the kick.
10. The arm is free of tension on the shuto. Pull back the opposite arm hard as you shuto and try to touch the shoulder blades together.
11. The block before the last awase uke is chudan uke. This block is a form of mawashi uke. The closed fists turn as in the open hand version.
12. As awase zuki is completed, the fists twist in to focus the punch.

Gekisai Dai Ichi Kata

Gekisai Dai Ichi Bunkai:

1. Tori attacks seiken zuki jodan. Uke blocks with jodan, then steps in and strikes seiken zuki jodan to nose or throat.
2. Tori kicks mae geri chudan. Uke shifts into shiko dachi at 45° while blocking gedan hara uke. Uke then counters with gyaku zuki while shifting into zenkutsu dachi.
3. Tori attacks seiken zuki chudan. Uke blocks chudan yoko uke and counters with mae geri to groin, followed by hiji ate to solar plexus process and then back fists tori's face. Tori then attacks seiken zuki gedan. Uke blocks gedan barai and counters with seiken zuki gedan to tanden, especially the bladder.
4. Tori attacks chudan seiken zuki. Uke uses sabaki to get to the outside, then sweeps the front foot and performs shuto uke at the same time while grasping the striking arm with hiki uke. Uke then strikes shuto uchi to throat and applies arm bar.
5. Tori attacks chudan zuki. Uke blocks chudan yoko uke and then strikes awase zuki and pushes.

Gekisai Dai Ichi Continuous Bunkai:

Seikichi Toguchi Sensei developed Gekisai Dai Ichi Continuous Bunkai. It is a special bunkai done with Gekisai Dai Ichi with two karate-kas working together through the whole performance of the kata. As the name implies, it is nonstop until the kata is finished. It is a unique way of training, which is invigorating and educational. It takes thought at first, but as students progress, speed and power are increased. There are now several slight variations on this drill. I prefer a hybrid of the International Organization of Goju Ryu Karate (IOGKF) version and Sensei Toguchi's original version. Only a few descriptors will be given here to help give some idea of what this drill looks like.

Gekisai Dai Ichi Continuous Bunkai Descriptors

Uke performs the kata (with *slight variation*) and Tori attacks and block in the appropriate manner. *Uke steps backward on each chudan yoko uke.* Uke kicks twice. *Uke uses his back foot to sweep during the shuto ending with it in front.* Tori uses a gedan oshi barai as Uke kicks. Tori uses yoko shotei uke and then ko uke when Uke attacks with hiji ate and uraken uchi. Uke always wins and therefore finishes last.

Gekisai Dai Ni Kata

Gekisai Dai Ni Kata:

1. Bow, then from the yoi position, pivot into hidarai sanchin dachi and execute jodan age uke.
2. Step into migi han zenkutsu dachi, oi zuki jodan.
3. Step back into shiko dachi and block hidarai gedan hara uke.
4. Step into migi sanchin dachi, jodan age uke.
5. Step into hidarai han zenkutsu dachi, hidarai oi zuki.
6. Step back into shiko dachi and block migi gedan hara uke.
7. Step into hidarai sanchin dachi, hidarai hiki uke.
8. Step into migi sanchin dachi, migi kake uke.
9. Kick hidarai mae geri, age hiji ate, kiai, uraken uchi, gedan barai and gedan gyaku zuki.
10. Sweep with back leg and shuto.
11. Step through into hidarai sanchin dachi, hidarai hiki uke.
12. Step forward and back in a semi circle into sanchin dachi each time while performing hiki uke.
13. Kick migi mae geri, migi age hiji ate, kiai, uraken uchi, gedan barai, gedan gyaku zuki.
14. Sweep with the back foot and shuto.
15. Drop back 45° into migi neko ashi dachi, tora guchi.
16. Step straight across into hidarai neko ashi dachi, tora guchi.
17. Pivot forward.
18. Return to the yoi and bow.

Gekisai Dai Ni Kata Special Considerations:

1. Close shuto hand while pulling back.
2. On the shuto, make beginners emphasize the shuto then slide the arm across the throat.
3. The first hiki uke is done with muchimi, and the second and third are done quickly.
4. Top hand of tora guchi is slightly above the shoulder, and the bottom hand is just inside the knee.
5. Pull back hiki uke hard in a fist to add power to hiji ate.
6. Palms are tight and white.
7. Tora guchi can be used to grip, tear and push as well as strike.

Gekisai Dai Ni Kata

8. Focus on the outside part of the hands while doing tora guchi. The movements must be slow and with muchimi.
9. Suri ashi 45° to the rear on the first neko ashi and straight across to the second neko ashi. The second neko ashi is lower as you set.
10. The head, eyes, body and chudan yoko uke all move together.
11. Grip after kicking and pull back hard.

Gekisai Dai Ni Bunkai:

There are only two new standard bunkai introduced with this kata.

1. Tori attacks chudan seiken zuki. Uke blocks hiki uke from the outside, pulls and grabs tori's arm with the other hand and grabs Yubi Hasami to throat while stepping on tori's foot.
2. Tori attacks jodan seiken oi zuki, followed by gyaku zuki gedan. Uke opens tori up by blocking jodan and gedan. Uke then pushes tori with both hands.

Turning Sanchin Kata

Turning Sanchin Kata:

1. Bow, then from the yoi position, step into migi sanchin dachi and open into morote chudan yoko uke.

2. Breath in as you pull back hidari arm and breath out while striking hidari chudan zuki. Pull the punching hand back to chudan yoko uke after completion of the punch.

3. Step into hidari sanchin dachi and breath in as you pull back migi arm and breath out while striking migi chudan zuki. Pull the punching hand back to chudan yoko uke after completion of the punch.

4. Step into migi sanchin dachi and breath in as you pull back hidari arm and breath out while striking hidari chudan zuki. Breath in and pull the punching hand all the way back to chamber after completing the punch. Bring the migi arm across the body, cross the migi foot in front of the hidari foot, look hidari and turn 180° counterclockwise while executing chudan yoko uke and pulling the migi hand back to chamber. (After the turn be in hidari sanchin dachi with the migi hand in chamber).

5. Breath out and execute migi chudan zuki. Breath in and pull the punching hand back to morote chudan yoko uke.

6. Step into migi sanchin dachi. Breath in, pulling the hidari hand back to chamber and breath out while punching hidari chudan zuki. Breath in while bringing the punching hand back to morote chudan yoko uke.

7. Step into hidari sanchin dachi. Breath, in pulling the migi hand back to chamber and breath out while punching migi chudan zuki. Breath in while bringing the punching hand back to morote chudan yoko uke.

8. Step into migi sanchin dachi and breath in as you pull back hidari arm and breath out while striking hidari chudan zuki. Breath in and pull the punching hand all the way back to chamber after completing the punch. Bring the migi arm across the body, cross the migi foot in front of the hidari foot, look hidari and turn 180° counterclockwise while executing chudan yoko uke and pulling the migi hand back to chamber. (After the turn be in hidari sanchin dachi with the migi hand in chamber).

9. Step into migi sanchin dachi. Breath in, pulling the hidari hand back to chamber and breath out while punching hidari chudan zuki. Breath in while bringing the punching hand back to morote chudan yoko uke.

10. Step into migi sanchin dachi. Breath in, pulling the hidari hand back to chamber and breath out while punching hidari chudan zuki. Breath in while bringing the punching hand back to morote chudan yoko uke.

11. Step into migi sanchin dachi and breath in as you pull back hidari arm and breath out while striking hidari chudan zuki. Leave the striking hand

out. Open both hands, rotate the palms and press down forming a semicircle with the arms.

12. Grip with both hands, starting with the index finger. Rotate the fists and pull them both back to chamber. Strike morote nukite chudan forming a semicircle with the arms. Repeat for a total of three pulls. Leave the hands out on the last nukite.

13. Step backward into hidari sanchin dachi and execute tora guchi.

14. Return to yoi position and bow.

Turning Sanchin Kata Special Considerations:

1. Breathing is slightly faster than Miyagi Chojun Sensei's version.

2. A simple way to remember the pattern is to step, punch 3 times, then turn punch, returning to morote chudan yoko uke, and step. Do the same sequence again but with one more hidari punch after the last step. Grip and pull 3 times. Only execute one tora guchi.

Turning Sanchin Bunkai:

None specified here.

Saifa Kata

Saifa Kata:

1. Bow, then from yoi step 45° into migi zenkutsu dachi, stand into musubi dachi while grasping right fist with left hand, push migi hand across chest, drop back into shiko dachi block head and chest with left hand and strike migi uraken zuki.
2. Repeat it on other side.
3. Repeat again with same side as number one
4. While looking to migi, block sukui uke hidari and gedan shotei uke migi while doing migi hiza geri.
5. Continue looking migi while kicking keage migi mae geri.
6. Perform the same technique on the other side.
7. Drop back into migi zenkutsu dachi and punch morote seiken zuki to collar bone.
8. Migi tettsui uchi into palm of hidarai.
9. Cross the front leg and turn into hidarai zenkutsu dachi while reaching under and blocks hidarai hiki uke and strike morote seiken zuki to collar bone level.
10. Hidarai tettsui uchi into palm of migi.
11. Sweep with rear foot while striking migi tettsui uchi to top of head. Kiai.
12. Grab, pull and strike.
13. Repeat on other side.
14. Step through migi, with small migi pressing block.
15. Strike hidarai gyaku zuki.
16. Turn into migi neko ashi dachi, perform tora guchi.
17. Return to the yoi position and bow.

Saifa Kata Special Considerations:

1. Chamber hand pulls back hard at the completion of tettsui uchi.
2. Right arm reaches high and back before last haito zuki.

Saifa Kata

Saifa Bunkai:

1. Tori grabs uke's wrist. Uke steps 45° and breaks the hold by pulling with both hands. Tori then strikes with oi zuki. Uke steps back into shiko dachi, blocks osae uke and counters with ude uchi to tori's face.
2. Tori strikes chudan zuki followed by mae geri. Uke blocks tori's strike with sukui uke and tori's kick with shotei gedan barai and hold on to the kick. Uke then executes hiza geri to tori's groin followed by a mae geri with the same leg.
3. Tori attacks with morote ubi basami to uke's neck. Uke blocks morote hiki uke, retains the arms, head butts tori, and executes morote seiken zuki chudan.
4. Tori tries to grab uke's leg for a take down. Uke defends by executing yoko tettsui uchi to tori's temple and twists tori's head rolling him to the ground. Uke finishes with strikes to the eyes with both thumbs.
5. Tori attacks chudan zuki. Uke pivots 90° and blocks with a swinging ude uke. The block follows through into tettsui uchi to tori's head. Uke then grabs tori's hair, pulls down and strikes ura zuki to tori's face.
6. Tori attack chudan zuki. Uke side steps 45°, blocks hiki uke and strikes haito uchi to tori's neck, or kidneys (depending on the height of the attacker) or both.
7. Tori attacks jodan seiken oi zuki, followed by gyaku zuki gedan. Uke reaches across and blocks jodan, then reaches across and blocks gedan and grabs. Uke then bends the gedan punch up, breaks the arm, and does takedown.

Seiyunchin Kata

Seiyunchin Kata:

1. Bow, then from yoi position step into migi shiko dachi at a 45° angle while brining the hands to osae uke at ganka level.

2. Bring the hands downward in a circular motion. At the bottom of the circle, place the hands back to back and bring them up to chin level. Grip the hands into fists and bring them down into morote gedan hara uke. Bring the hidari hand, open and palm up, to chamber while performing sukui uke with the migi hand. Execute nukite with the hidarai hand while pulling the migi hand back to chamber.

3. Step into hidari shiko dachi at 45° and repeat #2 using the opposite side.

4. Step into migi shiko dachi at 45° angle and repeat #2.

5. Roll the migi hand into a fist and bring it across the hidari palm.

6. Sabaki forward into migi neko ashi dachi and punch migi chudan zuki while keeping the hidari palm over the fist.

7. Step back into hidari neko ashi dachi, bring the migi hand back and then strike migi hiji ate into the hidari palm.

8. Step into migi renoji dachi while performing augmented migi chudan yoko uke.

9. Shift into hidari shiko dachi and execute hidari gedan barai.

10. Shift back into migi shiko dachi and execute migi gedan barai.

11. Step up into hidari renoji dachi while performing augmented hidari chudan yoko uke.

12. Shift into migi shiko dachi and execute migi gedan barai.

13. Shift back into hidari shiko dachi and execute hidari gedan barai.

14. Drop back into migi shiko dachi while performing archer block (hari uke; open hand gedan barai and open hand jodan uke, together)

15. Drop back into hidari shiko dachi while performing archer block (hari uke; open hand gedan barai and open hand jodan uke, together)

16. Sabaki forward into migi heiko dachi while executing chudan ude uchi into hidari palm.

17. Sabaki forward and deliver uraken uchi jodan.

18. Bring the migi foot across in front of the hidari foot, dropping low, and turn while executing joge uke.

19. Drop into migi shiko dachi while executing migi age zuki (with kiai), uraken uchi and gedan barai. The hidari hand stays in front of solar plexus.

20. Shift back to hidari shiko dachi and execute hidari gedan barai.

21. Move the back foot to center and back while dropping into migi neko ashi dachi and delivering migi hiji ate and hidari ushiro hiji ate.

Seiyunchin Kata

22. Move backward into hidari neko ashi dachi while delivering migi hiji ate and hidari ushiro hiji ate.
23. Bring the hidari (front) foot across in bensoku dachi and turn while executing joge uke.
24. Drop into hidari shiko dachi while executing hidari age zuki (with kiai), uraken uchi and gedan barai. The migi hand stays in front of solar plexus.
25. Shift back into migi shiko dachi and perform migi gedan barai.
26. Move the back foot back and to center while dropping into hidari neko ashi dachi while performing hidari hiji ate and ushiro hiji ate.
27. Move backward into migi neko ashi dachi while performing hidari hiji ate and ushiro hiji ate.
28. Sabaki forward into heiko dachi while executing migi uraken uchi and hidari shotei otoshi uke.
29. Slide a long step back into hidari neko ashi dachi while bringing both arms back and up. Then turn them back-to-back while dropping into neko ashi dachi and brining the arms down to yama uke (aka kuri uke).
30. Return to yoi position and bow.

Seiyunchin Kata Special Considerations:

1. Deep shiko dachi on archer block.
2. Nukite out at 45° angle.
3. Leave hand out in front of solar plexus during age zuki and gedan barai.
4. Bring thumbs across ribs and up turning elbows out, in and out again.
5. Hands should form a 90° angle at end of kata.
6. Renoji dachi, line heel up with instep and be one and a half foot distance out leaning slightly forward.
7. Thumb inside forearm on first uraken uchi.

Seiyunchin Kata

Seiyunchin Bunkai:

1. Tori attacks by grabbing uke's throat with both hands. Uke grabs tori's wrists from the inside. Uke then pulls them down and back toward his hips and twists. Uke then delivers three hiza geris.

2. Tori attacks oi zuki chudan. Uke blocks sukui uke under the elbow. Uke then pulls tori forward using hiki uke and executes nukite to tori's floating rib.

3. Tori attacks chudan zuki. Uke blocks using osae uke then strikes naka daka ippon ken to solar plexus. Uke immediately grabs the back of tori's head and follows through with hiji ate.

4. Tori attacks chudan zuki. Uke blocks chudan yoko uke and strikes tori's jaw with shotei uke then shifts into shiko dachi and strikes tettsui uchi to groin.

5. Tori attacks oi zuki jodan. Uke blocks jodan hiki uke, and maintains arm. Tori strikes mae geri. Uke scoops the kick and throws tori to the ground.

6. Tori attacks chudan zuki. Uke blocks using opposite shotei otoshi uke and maintains grip on arm. Uke blocks using uchi uke, shifts forward, pulls tori and strikes uraken uchi to tori's face.

7. Tori attacks chudan zuki and mae geri. Uke blocks joge uke and counters with age zuki uraken uchi and tettsui uchi to groin.

8. Tori sets in with a strong bear hug from behind uke.. Uke pushes his shoulders forward, digs his right fist between his chest and tori's arm and brings his right elbow up with a fast motion and executes a powerful strike with his left elbow to tori's solar plexus. Uke then shifts forward, turns and strikes chudan zuki.

9. Tori attacks chudan zuki. Uke blocks osae uke and counters with uraken uchi.

10. Tori attacks morote zuki to chudan level. Uke blocks using morote hiji kuri uke, executes morote shuto uchi to tori's neck, grabs tori's head and knees him in the face.

Tensho Kata

Tensho Kata:

1. Bow, then from the yoi position open into migi sanchin dachi and morote chudan yoko uke.
2. Breathe in while pulling the hidari hand back to chamber. Exhale strongly upon completion.
3. Breathe in while executing migi jodan hiki uke and migi haishu (backhand) kake uke.
4. Breathe out while executing migi jodan shotei oshi (push).
5. Breathe in and execute migi jodan ura te kake uke while pulling the migi hand back to chamber.
6. Breathe out and execute migi gedan shotei oshi.
7. Breathe in and execute migi chudan ko uke.
8. Breathe out and execute migi chudan shotei otoshi uke.
9. Breathe in and execute migi chudan yoko ko uke.
10. Breathe out and execute migi chudan uchi shotei uke.
11. Step into hidari sanchin dachi, pulling the migi hand back to chamber, and execute hidari chudan yoko uke.
12. Repeat #3-#10 on hidari side.
13. Step into migi sanchin dachi and morote chudan yoko uke.
14. Repeat #3-#10 using both hands.
15. Step back into hidari sanchin dachi and execute morote osae uke.
16. Step back into migi sanchin dachi while executing morote sukui uke, then morote osae uke.
17. Step back into hidari sanchin dachi while executing tora guchi.
18. Step back into migi sanchin dachi while executing tora guchi.
19. Return to yoi position and bow.

Tensho Kata

Tensho Kata Special Considerations:

1. Ura uchi uke must block all the way to the middle.
2. Thumb is tight to the palm.
3. The shotei oshi finishes slightly higher than the shoulder.
4. Shotei oshi blocks to ganka point.
5. The inner forearm presses against the inside of the body.
6. Bend the knees to sink the body slightly when doing morote mae shotei oshi.
7. Turn the leading heel in slightly before stepping. The leading heel is the heel that is furthest from the body in the direction it is stepping whether it is forward or backward.
8. After morote shotei oshi, step backward and press down strongly with the palm.
9. Tensho has two tora guchi to emphasize the importance of learning to move backward.
10. In order to regulate breathing after the kata is completed, try the following exercise: Extend the arms straight out from the shoulders. As you breath in, bring the shoulders and upper back up to the neck. As you exhale, stretch them out to the sides. Repeat this several times.

Tensho Kata Bunkai:

None specified here.

Shisochin Kata

Shisochin Kata:

1. Bow, then from yoi position open into migi sanchin dachi and morote chudan nukite no kamae. Then deliver a hidari nukite and bring it back to chudan nukite no kamae.

2. Step into hidari sanchin dachi and deliver a migi nukite brining it back to chudan nukite no kamae.

3. Step into migi sanchin dachi and deliver a hidari nukite and bring it back to chudan nukite no kamae.

4. Bring the hands together by touching the shuto edges. Grip them into fists, starting with the small finger, and quickly bring them down to morote gedan barai while stepping back into hidari zenkutsu dachi.

5. Step forward at 45° into migi zenkutsu dachi while executing migi ura chudan kake uke and kaisho gedan barai. Bring the hidari hand under the migi elbow, at the same time, in a circular pattern, execute hidari hiki uke and migi osae hiki uke pulling both hand back to the chamber on the migi side with the hidari hand under the migi. Then turn the hips so as to be in hidari zenkutsu dachi and deliver ude osae (similar to hiji ate) and bring the hidari hand back to chamber with it open and down.

6. Step forward into hidari zenkutsu dachi at a 45° angle and repeat the opposite of #5.

7. Step into heisoku dachi by bringing the hidari foot forward. Pull the hips in then thrust them out while delivering migi age hiji ate and hidari ushiro hiji ate.

8. Turn counterclockwise 180° into hidari zenkutsu dachi (by dropping the migi foot back). At the same time, execute hidari jodan shotei zuki and migi gedan shotei barai.

9. Turn clockwise 180° into migi zenkutsu dachi (by brining the hidari foot over slightly while turning) At the same time, execute migi jodan shotei zuki and hidari gedan shotei barai.

10. Pivot 90° counterclockwise into hidari zenkutsu dachi. At the same time, execute hidari jodan shotei zuki and migi gedan shotei barai.

11. Turn clockwise 180° into migi zenkutsu dachi (by bringing the hidari foot over slightly while turning) At the same time, execute migi jodan shotei zuki and hidari gedan shotei barai.

12. Step into hidari sanchin dachi while executing hidari chudan yoko uke.

13. Kick migi mae geri, landing in migi zenkutsu dachi and deliver migi hiji ate, bring the hidari hand in front of the solar plexus. Kiai.

14. Turn 180° counterclockwise into hidari sanchin dachi while performing hidari chudan hiki uke.

Shisochin Kata

15. Step into migi sanchin dachi while performing migi hiki uke.
16. Execute hidari mae geri, landing in hidari zenkutsu dachi while delivering hidari hiji ate and pulling the migi palm in front of the solar plexus. Kiai.
17. Pivot 90° clockwise into migi zenkutsu dachi. The hidari hand executes shotei osae uke and the migi hand executes hiji ate.
18. Turn 180° counterclockwise into hidari neko ashi dachi and morote chudan ura kake uke.
19. Step into migi zenkutsu dachi while grabbing, pulling and delivering morote hiji ate.
20. Step forward into hidari zenkutsu dachi at a 45° angle and repeat the opposite of #21.
21. Step forward at 45° into migi zenkutsu dachi while executing migi ura chudan kake uke and kaisho gedan barai. Bring the hidari hand under the migi elbow, at the same time, in a circular pattern, execute hidari hiki uke and migi osae hiki uke pulling both hand back to the chamber on the migi side with the hidari hand under the migi. Then turn the hips so as to be in hidari zenkutsu dachi and deliver ude osae (similar to hiji ate) and bring the hidari hand back to chamber with it open and down.
22. Step into heisoku dachi by bringing the migi foot forward. Pull the hips in then thrust them out while delivering migi age hiji ate and hidari ushiro hiji ate.
23. Step forward and turn 180° counterclockwise into hidari neko ashi dachi and execute migi chudan ura kake uke and hidari kaisho gedan barai.
24. Bring the hands together. Return to the yoi position and bow.

Shisochin Kata Special Considerations:

1. Pause after striking backward.
2. Both hiki uke are fast.
3. Step and turn quickly at end.
4. Arms form 90° angle while pulling down and back.
5. Start with small finger on the first grip.
6. Pull hands quickly back into diamond, pause, then quickly into arm bar while squeezing biceps and using hip.
7. Both hands up before morote haito uke.
8. Arm slightly in front of groin in a natural bend.
9. Nukite is slightly up while pulling back and down and up while striking. They are done quickly out and back.
10. Press shoulder blades together when pulling back.

Shisochin Kata

11. Bottom hand up while in chamber for haito.
12. Step out in 45° zenkutsu dachi so you will be shoulder width apart for arm break. No sliding.
13. Make hand into a diamond before arm break and don't pull too far back.
14. Stand before striking ushiro hiji ate.
15. Very deep and long zenkutsu dachi.
16. Set heel down, grip and pull.

Shisochin Bunkai:

1. Tori strikes seiken zuki. Uke blocks gyaku zuki with open hand hidarai chudan yoko uke and strike solar plexus with migi nukite.
2. Tori executes a double grab to uke's neck. Uke blocks morote open hand chudan uke, executes morote shuto uchi, grabs tori's ears and rips them off.
3. Tori does a double grab to forearms of uke. Uke pushes up then brings down quickly with knee strike.
4. Tori strikes seiken zuki. Uke blocks open hand chudan yoko uke and open hand strike to groin on inside of tori. Ukes turns and arm bars tori while stepping through to off balance him.
5. Tori grabs uke from behind. Uke strikes hidarai ushiro hiji uchi and migi ushiro seiken zuki (over shoulder as in kata).
6. Tori kicks migi mae geri. Uke blocks with hidarai shotei uke (keeping leg) while striking shotei to tori's face. Uke steps in placing migi foot behind tori's only leg throwing tori to the ground and finishes with a foot lock.
7. Tori steps in striking migi oi zuki chudan. Uke blocks open hand hidarai chudan yoko uke, kicks mae geri and strikes hiji ate. Uke then strikes tori's face with open hand grip and pushes.
8. Tori strikes migi chudan zuki. Uke blocks down hidarai osae uke, strikes hiji ate, and then strikes Tori's face with open hand tettsui uchi and pushes tori back.
9. Tori steps in and executes a double grab to uke's throat. Uke's blocks morote open hand chudan uke, slams open hands down on tori's shoulders, grabs the gi, turns fists upward and head buts tori. Uke then strikes otoshi hiji ate and morote yoko hiji and pushes chest.
10. Tori attacks Uke with migi gedan zuki. Uke blocks hidari gedan uke open hand. Uke's migi hand scoops under Tori's striking arm, comes up and leverages Tori to the ground in arm lock.

Sanseru Kata

Sanseru Kata:

1. Bow, then from yoi position open into migi sanchin dachi and morote chudan yoko uke. Pull the hidari hand back and deliver chudan zuki pulling it back to chudan yoko uke.
2. Step into hidari sanchin dachi and deliver migi chudan zuki pulling it back to chudan yoko uke.
3. Step into migi sanchin dachi and deliver hidari chudan zuki leaving the fist extended.
4. Open the migi fist and press the palm outward while pulling the hidari fist back to chamber.
5. Drop the migi foot back into hidari zenkutsu dachi while clasping the migi arm with the hidari hand and pulling back to chamber with the migi arm as the hidari hand slides down and off the arm.
6. Step into migi zenkutsu dachi while scooping with the migi hand striking shotei with the hidari hand, leaving the hand extended.
7. Kick hidari mae geri then migi mae geri very quickly with the hands maintaining their crossed position ending in migi zenkutsu dachi. Execute migi hiji ate and (without using the hips) hidari gedan zuki.
8. Execute migi kansetsu geri while leaving the hands in place.
9. Turn 180° by using the momentum from pulling the kick up and execute chudan yoko uke landing in hidari sanchin dachi.
10. Kick migi mae geri and deliver migi hiji ate and (without using the hips) hidari gedan zuki landing in migi zenkutsu dachi.
11. Execute migi kansetsu geri while leaving the hands in place.
12. Turn 90° by using the momentum from pulling the kick up and execute chudan yoko uke landing in hidari sanchin dachi.
13. Kick migi mae geri and deliver migi hiji ate and (without using the hips) hidari gedan zuki landing in migi zenkutsu dachi.
14. Execute migi kansetsu geri while leaving the hands in place.
15. Turn 180° by using the momentum from pulling the kick up and execute chudan yoko uke landing in hidari sanchin dachi.
16. Kick migi mae geri and deliver migi hiji ate and (without using the hips) hidari gedan zuki, landing in migi zenkutsu dachi.
17. Pivot into shiko dachi and execute, migi over hidari, gedan kosa uke.
18. Step clockwise into shiko dachi and execute, hidari over migi, haishu gedan kosa uke.
19. Sabaki counterclockwise into shiko dachi and execute migi yoko kaisho jodan uke while pulling the hidari hand palm up under the migi pectoral.
20. Sabaki into migi heiko dachi and deliver awase zuki. Kiai.

Sanseru Kata

21. Turn counterclockwise 180° into hidari sanchin dachi while executing hidari chudan yoko uke.

22. Step forward into migi sanchin dachi and execute migi chudan yoko uke.

23. Step into shiko dachi and execute hidari yoko kaisho jodan uke while pulling the migi hand palm up under the hidari pectoral.

24. Sabaki into hidari heiko dachi and deliver awase zuki. Kiai.

25. Turn clockwise 270° into shiko dachi. At the same time as the turn, turn the hidari wrist inside, cross the arms (migi inside hidari) twist them inward and execute morote ko uke.

26. Turn the front foot in slightly and bring the hand together. Return to the yoi position and bow.

Sanseru Kata Special Considerations:

1. Foot back almost as in neko before morote zuki (a modified heiko dachi).

2. Curl hand up before archer block.

3. Keep back straight lean forward, down and back up while scooping.

4. Pull toes back and use heel, not locking out the knee, while doing kansetsu geri at a 45° angle. Also bend the supporting leg and

5. Keep head the same height while kicking mae geri.

6. Fast then slow on chudan yoko uke as if you've been hit, recovering and moving forward.

7. Circular movement after archer block.

8. Bring hand across while rolling and gripping at the same time with the other hand.

9. Always have hands together before stepping and ending kata.

10. Come up in the stance before kosa uke in shiko.

11. Grip with index finger first, leave hand out and don't pull back until after grip.

12. Get hands to cross while doing mae geri.

13. Leg up before turn, use downward momentum to turn.

14. Extend morote zuki

Sanseru Kata

Sanseru Kata Bunkai:

1. Tori punches migi oi zuki chudan. Uke blocks down hard with hidarai chudan yoko uke and strikes Tori in solar plexus. 1a. Double punch, double block.
2. Tori grabs Uke's right hand with his left hand. Uke lifts and turns his hand while striking down with his left hand to free the grab while turning to the side and executing shuto Tori's head
3. Tori kicks mae geri. Uke grabs kicking leg, kicks groin then turns his kicking leg taking Tori to the ground and finishing in a foot lock.
4. Tori strikes migi oi zuki. Uke blocks gedan (osae uke is okay) kicks, strikes migi hiji ate. Uke punches gedan then steps to the side executes kansetsu geri pulling Tori to the ground. Uke can finish with a shuto to the back of Tori's neck.
5. Tori strikes jodan and kicks gedan. Uke blocks jodan and gedan maintaining hold of Tori. Uke then turns Tori and takes Tori to the ground striking morote zuki.
6. Tori strikes migi oi zuki. Uke blocks hidarai yoko uke. Tori strikes jodan gyaku zuki. Uke blocks migi jodan ko uke, steps in strikes eyes, drops and takes Tori down to ground with knee grab (hand that is on top stays on top).

Seipai Kata

Seipai Kata:

1. Bow, then from the yoi position drop back 90° into migi shiko dachi while moving the open hidari hand in a circle close to the body in front of the face, ending at solar plexus, and moving the open migi hand in a large circle above the head ending with the arm slightly bent and fingers in front of the face at eye level.

2. Step into hidari heiko dachi while bringing the hidari palm in up in a scooping motion from hip level and clasping it with the migi palm in front of the solar plexus (palms are horizontal).

3. Step into migi han zenkutsu dachi while drawing the hands inward during the step and then delivering a clasped hand strike when finished ending with hidari palm on top.

4. Pivot on the heels into migi shiko dachi while dropping the hips. Keep the hands clasped striking migi hiji ate, keeping the hidari elbow close to the body.

5. Step into hidari kokutsu dachi while performing hidari gedan shotei barai beginning just above the elbow joint on the migi arm. Pull the migi arm back hard ending with it palm down next to the migi shoulder. Then, perform hidari chudan haishu mawashi osae uke in front of the face ending at shoulder level.

6. Pivot into hidari zenkutsu dachi while delivering migi jodan shuto uchi and puling the hidari palm back to the side ending with the hidari palm forward.

7. Execute migi mae geri (keeping the hands the same) then drop back into hidari shiko dachi while executing migi ushiro hiji ate, hidari hiji ate and hidari uraken uchi.

8. Turn 90° clockwise into migi neko ashi dachi while performing migi gedan barai with the hidari fist under the migi elbow palm down. Execute migi chudan yoko uke and migi hiki uke.

9. Turn clockwise 180° into migi heiko dachi while brining the hidari open hand, palm out, in front of the forehead and down to the waist level. At the same time bring the migi open hand in front of the chest with the palm twisting inward then raising and twisting outward. Then execute migi suihei osae and hidari maki age ending with the migi hand palm down and closed below the hidari hand which is palm up and closed.

10. Turn counterclockwise 225° (180°+45°) into migi heiko dachi. Simultaneously while turning open the hands raising the hidari hand over the head ending in haishu uke in chamber. At the same time execute a groin slap with the migi hand.

Chapter 6: Kata and Bunkai

Seipai Kata

11. Slide into hidari renoji dachi while executing hidari gedan harai uke and migi shotei oshi.

12. Step into migi shiko dachi moving the hands in front of the abdomen into morote ninoji ganae. Pull both hands back into chamber. Perform migi ashi barai fumikomi while striking morote ryoken naka daka ippon ken gedan zuki with kiai.

13. Step back clockwise into hidari shiko dachi while delivering hidari gedan harai uke.

14. Slide 90° into migi renoji dachi while executing migi gedan harai uke and hidari shotei oshi.

15. Only turn 90° clockwise then repeat the rest of 10,11,12 and 13 on the opposite side of body and turning the opposite direction.

16. Shift the migi foot back (so the body faces the front) into hidari neko ashi dachi while executing hidari chudan yoko uke and migi jodan furi zuki.

17. Slide the right foot forward into migi bensoku dachi while executing migi chudan yoko uke and hidari jodan furi zuki.

18. Pivot counterclockwise 270° into hidari heiko dachi while executing hidari hiki uke.

19. Pivot 90° clockwise into migi heiko dachi while executing hidari heiken uchi then immediately deliver hidari jodan uraken uchi.

20. Pivot counterclockwise 90° into hidari heiko dachi while performing migi chudan yoko uke. Execute migi mae geri.

21. Drop the foot back into hidari shiko dachi while executing hidari ura zuki bringing the migi open hand in front of the solar plexus.

22. Repeat 19, 20 and 21 on the opposite side of body and turning the opposite direction.

23. Slide the hidari foot back into migi neko ashi dachi while executing ninoji no kamae with the migi hand on top.

24. Slide a long step back into hidari neko ashi dachi while executing mawashi uke and pull. Execute morote gedan uchi brining the migi fist into the palm of the hidari hand with kiai.

25. Bring the hidari foot back into musubi dachi.

26. Return to yoi position and bow.

Seipai Kata Special Considerations

1. The migi arm and hidari leg are in a line while in kokutsu dachi.
2. Turn the fists while executing hiji ate.
3. Uraken is at nose level so not to obstruct vision.

Seipai Kata

4. Turn the forearm in while blocking down and out when blocking chudan.
5. Don't lift feet off the floor while turning.
6. Lower slightly while sliding in renoji dachi.
7. Try to keep both heels on the ground in bensoku dachi.
8. Snap the wrist while executing heiken uchi keeping the thumb to the side.
9. Bring the thumb across the fist as you strike uraken uchi jodan.
10. Pull the elbows down hard and push the hips forward just before morote gedan uchi.

Seipai Kata Bunkai:

1. Tori grabs Uke's wrist. Uke breaks the hold by brining the free hand up hard against Tori's wrist. Uke continues through and strikes Tori with jodan otoshi shuto uchi on the nose.
2. Tori kicks uke with migi leg. Uke scoops up the leg with hidari hand and clasps it with migi hand. Uke then pushes both hands forward, turning and throwing Tori.
3. Tori grabs with his hidari hand Uke's migi hand. Uke turns his migi hand palm up and circles around back of Tori. Uke clasps his hands together, pulls back and chokes Tori.
4. Tori grabs with his migi hand Uke's migi hand. Uke steps back into kokutsu dachi wiping off Tori's grip with the free hand. Tori strikes hidari choku zuki. Uke blocks with his hidari backhand as in kata. He then executes shuto uchi, mae geri, twists Tori's head to the ground and executes uraken uchi to Tori's face.
5. Tori kicks migi mae geri and follows with migi chudan zuki. Uke blocks with gedan harai uke and chudan hiki uke. Uke then grabs Tori's wrist turns clockwise and winds the hidari hand around Tori's arm, locking it. Torus tries to escape by clasping his hand together and pulling back. Uke turns and strikes Tori in the groin.
6. Tori kicks with his hidari leg. Uke blocks and scoops with his hidari hand and shifts to the outside of Tori. Uke grabs Tori's hair and pulls back while lifting Tori's leg. Uke also sweeps the supporting leg, throwing Tori to the ground.
7. Tori attacks with hidari chudan oi zuki. Uke shifts forward and to the outside as he blocks with a powerful hidari chudan yoko uke and simultaneously delivers migi jodan furi zuki
8. Tori strikes hidari chudan zuki. Uke block migi hiki uke. With the same hand Uke turns 90° clockwise grabs Tori's groin, and executes uraken uchi to Toris face. Tori punches choku zuki. Uke blocks chudan zuki, kicks mae geri, sets foot back, pulling Tori into ura zuki.
9. Tori kicks mae geri. Uke grabs the kick and pulls Tori off Balance by pulling him forward. Uke then turns the foot, throwing Tori to the ground and executes tettsui uchi to Tori's foot.

Original Open Hand Sanchin Kata

In February 2001, Sensei Wilson trained five days with, a 90-year-old Okinawan, Jin'an Matsumura Sensei. Jin'an Matsumura Sensei was a direct student of Miyagi Chojun Sensei in the 1930's. During the training, he taught Sensei Wilson the original open-hand version of Sanchin. Sensei Wilson taught the kata to me in March 2001. Matsumura Sensei passed away at the end of April 2001. It is truly a great honor and responsibility to be part of such a legacy.

Original Open Hand Sanchin Kata:

1. Bow.
2. Open into morote hiki uke, migi sanchin dachi.
3. Pull hidarai hand back and execute nukite gedan with wheezing breath.
4. Step into hidarai sanchin dachi, pull migi hand back and execute nukite gedan with wheezing breath.
5. Step into migi sanchin dachi, pull hidari hand back and execute nukite gedan with wheezing breath.
6. Turn 180° counterclockwise into hidarai sanchin dachi and at the same time execute mawashi uke hard and fast with hands ending to center.
7. Without stepping, go to morote hiki uke.
8. Pull migi hand back and execute nukite in hidarai sanchin dachi.
9. Step and repeat three more times (four times including the turn).
10. Turn 180° counterclockwise (finish facing the front) while doing mawashi uke hard and fast with hands ending to center.
11. Without stepping, go to morote hiki uke.
12. Pull migi hand back and execute nukite gedan then step into migi sanchin dachi.
13. Do one more hidarai nukite gedan without stepping.
14. Perform three morote nukite and stick them
15. Step back into hidari sanchin dachi and execute mawashi uke with hands to center.
16. Step back into migi sanchin dachi and execute mawashi uke with hands to center.
17. Bow.

Original Open Hand Sanchin Kata Special Considerations:

1. After each nukite return to morote hiki uke.
2. Keep the chin down and in, eyes forward and shoulders down and back.
3. Keep the heels of the feet in contact with the floor.

Original Open Hand Sanchin Kata Bunkai: None specified here.

Oyo Bunkai

Oyo Bunkai is application of the kata in ways other than the standard bunkai. Oyo Bunkai can be different for each individual. It comes about after long practice of the kata and standard bunkai. Different attempts at applications will be made successfully and unsuccessfully. This author recommends writing down the successful attempts and developing a large bank of oyo bunkai. Some thoughts to keep in mind while doing this is to vary the attacks which the tori uses. Look for throws, breaks, and chokes. Using different fist formations can change the application dramatically. Study and research will reveal a lot more! Students can record some oyo bunkai here.

Gekisai Dai Ichi Kata Oyo Bunkai

_____

_____

Gekisai Dai Ni Kata Oyo Bunkai

_____

_____

Saifa Kata Oyo Bunkai

_____

_____

Seyunchin Kata Oyo Bunkai

_____

_____

Shisochin Kata Oyo Bunkai

_____

_____

Sanseru Kata Oyo Bunkai

_____

_____

_____

Kata and Bunkai

<u>**Notes**</u>

Chapter 7

Kakie

Chapter 7 Table of Contents

Introduction

Kakie is thought by some to be the way to truly understand kumite. There are some sequential pointers to keep in mind when practicing. Beginners just need to go up and down back and forth. Later, begin to do more of a circular movement. Next, add body shifting and moving around the floor. Later, add techniques such as grabs, pushes and throws while standing. Then, do them while moving. At all times, use the non-pushing hand to protect the face in case tori's arm slips. Also try to make the breathing so it is not audible. Try to feel the opponent's energy. Always push your elbow in and out similar to Sanchin Kata, keeping it close to the body.

Another way to do kakie is with both hands. Both partners lock their wrists, one on the inside and one on the outside. The hands of the one on the inside are facing down and the hands of the one on the outside are facing up. Both people rotate their palms inside and switch positions but never lose contact. Press out, keeping elbows in, like Tensho Kata. This can be done with only one hand as well. Counters are not done with this.

Kakie can be done with two tori. The toris need to switch sides so both of their arms are developed. Counters that can be done against two tori include double groin strikes, double clothesline and banging their heads together. Getting to the outside and pushing both tori works too.

A completely different way of looking at kakie is to try and counter and reverse the locking techniques used. This takes knowledge of the techniques and is taught at a more advanced level. The following kakie techniques are only meant as notes and may not make sense without further instruction in the dojo.

Kakie Techniques

1. Grab throat with pushing hand while pulling tori's pushing arm with the other.

2. Step through and clothesline.

3. Step around back and choke.

4. Push chin and pull head, breaking neck.

5. Grab pushing hand on the way back, lock tori's elbow over his shoulder and throw.

6. Open tori up by blocking his pushing arm with uke's chamber arm, then push with one or both hands (the push can be done up, down, or straight).

7. Lock tori's pushing arm and bring it around back so it is in the L position.

8. As in Shisochin Kata, pull tori's pushing arm and place him in an arm bar taking him to the ground.

9. Use tori's wrist by catching it, then bend it back and take him down (both inside and outside).

10. Open tori and slide down grabbing both legs, push with head and take down.

11. Throw from inside and outside position as in Shisochin Kata (This is my oyo bunkai. It may need further explanation in the dojo).

12. Pull and elbow strike.

13. Arm bar as in Seiyunchin Kata (This is my oyo bunkai. It may need further explanation in the dojo).

14. Arm break over shoulder.

15. Open tori and elbow strike.

16. Pin front leg as in sanchin, trap and push.

17. Nukite to eyes while pulling tori's arm with your pushing hand.

18. Open tori and kick.

19. Open tori and gyaku zuki.

20. Open and head butt.

Kakie

Notes

Chapter 8
Kumite

Chapter 8 Table of Contents

Kumite

Introduction

Kumite takes confidence, endurance and perseverance. It can also be very confusing when you consider all its various forms. This chapter will try to explain an overview of kumite and give examples of drills when possible.

Kumite can be divided into two main categories: yakusoku and jiyu. Yakusoku translates as, "promise." This type of kumite is always prearranged and agreed upon between the participants. Jiyu translates as, "free." In this type of kumite, the participants can use whatever techniques they wish. However, sometimes the participants agree to exclude some techniques such as takedowns. Some of the various forms of kumite can be done both as yakusoku and jiyu. Each form in this paper is designated next to its name as to whether it is yakusoku, jiyu, or both.

Kumite can be learned by a variety of methods. These methods can be done progressively. First, bunkai develops speed, power and focus. At the same time, it develops a greater understanding of kata. Second, kotei ate (body conditioning) gets people used to taking punches and kicks. It is accurate to consider all yakusoku kumite as a form of kotei ate. Prearranged techniques should be delivered with force so both tori and uke can condition their bodies. Then, sanbon gi develops blocking, punching and countering techniques. Following this, form sparring develops free style flowing ability. Next, ippon kumite can develop both prearranged scenarios and spontaneous responses to spontaneous techniques. Then, yakusoku kumite can be used to focus on specific techniques with very lethal consequences. A high point in kumite training is jiyu kumite. This is often done with light contact. Han ju involves medium contact. Jiyu kumite can be done with takedowns, but often these are excluded. Lastly, iri kumi is done with heavy contact and takedowns. Liability is discussed in the last section of this chapter.

Bunkai (Yakusoku)

Bunkai deepens the students' understanding of kata and develops speed, power and focus. It can be done in beginning, intermediate and advanced stages These are known as kihon (basic), dento teki (traditional), and oyo (variations). In the beginning, pattern is emphasized. Later, speed and power are edeveloped. At all times, both tori and uke must kiai. By doing the bunkai on each side, both sides can be developed.

One way of doing standard bunkai is happo kumite, or circular bunkai. The person in the center does the bunkai against the other people quickly, almost as a continuous bunkai. This can also be adapted to fit a linear application. The tori can line up and the uke can move down the line performing each bunkai quickly and with full power. The uke then becomes the first person in line and the last person in line becomes the uke.

Another way of doing bunkai is to have one person do the kata completely, while the others are positioned to attack as techniques are being done. This helps people build a better visual picture of how the kata really works.

Continuous bunkai was developed by Taguchi Sensei and is a two person drill in which the kata is done as a nonstop bunkai. This was very creative of Taguchi Sensei. Specific bunkai is addressed in Chapter 6.

Kotei Ate

Kotei ate is done to toughen tissue and strengthen bone. A tonfa, or bo, can be used to work body parts individually. Partner (see ude and geri tanren) drills include kicking or slapping thighs in different stances, mainly in heiko dachi, sanchin dachi and shiko dachi. For beginners, their belts can be folded and used on themselves to condition different parts of the body. Advanced students might want to use a small (about one foot) closet dowel. Chishi and bo can be used for kotei ate individually or with partners. Other kotei ate drills, specifically ude tanren and geri tanren, are provided here.

Kotei Ate Drills: Ude Tanren and Geri Tanren

1. Chudan yoko, gedan barai, step and turn chudan yoko, gedan barai, shift into shiko dachi, gedan barai, gedan barai, repeat.
2. Five series (each component part can be broken down individually).
3. Tori strikes ushiro uraken uchi jodan while back is facing uke. Uke blocks jodan uke.
4. Tori strikes stomach of uke with mae geri (back leg from han zenkutsu) and tries to untie belt. Trade off kicks.
5. Partners trade off mawashi geri to thigh. Using the top of the foot hurts less for uke.
6. Lock legs in zenkutsu dachi and strike to stomach.
7. Jiyu kumite can be done very slowly and heavy giving each person a chance to give and receive heavy punches and kicks. Blocks are kept to a minimum.
8. Slam shoulders into one another while facing each other.
9. Tori pushes uke hard with both hands on uke's shoulders. Uke tries to step back but also absorbs the power and redirects it to the ground.
10. Kamae kumite can be practiced by locking the participants' front foot in shiko dachi (or other stances) and only using hands.
11. Open hand slapping of areas of the body.
12. Open hand partner drill where hands alternate a "high-five" with both the front and back of the hands.
13. Use Chishi on body.
14. Rolling tan on forearms.

Chapter 8: Kumite

Sanbon Gi (Yakusoku)

Sanbon gi is two-person combination kumite. It can be done with or without (sandan gi) stepping. It is often in a head, chest, down format (but can be chest, chest, chest, or head, head, head etc.). Initially this is done stepping in sanchin dachi but later it can be done stepping in zenkutsu dachi, shiko dachi or a combination of stances. The important thing to remember is to hit and block with 100% commitment.

If a prearranged final counter is to be used, then I recommend the last technique by tori be with a fourth strike and step (this may need to be called yonbon gi). This appears to be less confusing too, because a one, two, three, counter rhythm is easier to follow than a one, two, counter rhythm. (Perhaps this ease is only because of my familiarity with Toguchi Sensei's kiso kumite.)

I also recommend that students reset before going back the other way. This gives the instructor a chance to correct before starting again. I feel the best starting position is migi sanchin dachi and chudan yoko uke kamae. The partners need to be close enough so that the chest blocks can cross and make an "X". This way the distancing is correct. Switch the forward foot to the other side after ten repetitions. This works both sides.

Sanbon Gi Drills

1. Tori attacks head three times in sanchin dachi. The last (fourth) technique is to head. Uke blocks jodan age uke cross block in sanchin dachi and counters with seiken zuki to solar plexus.
2. Tori attacks chest three times in zenkutsu dachi. The last (fourth technique) to chest. Uke blocks chudan yoko uke in zenkutsu dachi with mae geri to groin with front leg.
3. Tori attacks gyaku zuki to head, chest, and down, stepping in sanchin dachi. Uke cross blocks appropriately in sanchin dachi. Tori's last (fourth) attack is with mae geri. Uke side steps to hidarai, blocking migi sukui uke and executes mae geri to tori with front leg.
4. Tori attacks gyaku zuki head, chest and down, stepping in sanchin, zenkutsu and shiko dachi. Tori's last (fourth) attack is gyaku zuki chudan in zenkutsu dachi. Uke cross blocks appropriately, stepping in the same stances. On the last attack, uke steps to the outside, blocks gedan uke and strikes tettsui uchi to the elbow, shoulder and head.
5. Tori attacks oi zuki head, chest and down in shiko dachi. The last (fourth) attack is oi zuki gedan in shiko dachi. Uke does the appropriate blocks in shiko dachi, and on the last attack, blocks tori's arm, slides behind the arm, down between tori's leg and flips tori forward by falling back.

Form Sparring (Jiyu)

Form sparring starts with tori attacking with a choku zuki. Uke blocks and does three counters. The last counter is done with a kiai and then roles are switched. The other person blocks the last technique and does three counters. The last counter is with a kiai and is left extended out, and so on. If a take down occurs, then the person who is standing lets the partner up and attacks with a choku zuki. Then it starts again. Over time, speed will increase and reactions will become more advanced. I have found the following form sparring drills useful as variations of form sparring.

Form Sparring Drills

1. Only use one arm and then only use the next arm. Then only one leg. Then only the next leg.
2. Only feet.
3. Only left side.
4. Only right side.
5. Use only techniques from Gekisai Dai Ichi (or another individual kata).
6. Dim lights and play loud music.
7. Outside on various terrain.
8. Focus shields on the floor as obstacles.

Ippon Kumite (Yakusoku and Jiyu)

In ippon (one point) kumite, tori does only one technique and uke usually does one block (or evasion) and counter. In ippon kumite, the techniques can be yakusoku (prearranged) or jiyu (at will, free techniques). In jiyu ippon kumite, uke does not know what or when an attack is going to occur. However, in jiyu practice, it may be best to limit the attack to one, two or three possibilities and/or provide a count, at least in the beginning.

It may be useful to try this first with a focus shield on the ground between the partners to provide distance. Then remove it. This builds confidence. One of the main points to remember is to develop getting to the side and to the back. Some ippon (yakusoku) and ippon (jiyu) kumite drills are listed here. Ippon yakusoku kumite is a good opportunity to practice stepping in and smothering attacks.

Ippon (Yakusoku) Kumite Drills

1. Tori attacks mawashi geri jodan. Uke does a double reinforced block and mae geri to groin.
2. Tori attacks mawashi geri to outside of uke's front leg. Uke lifts his leg up out of the way, grabs tori, and delivers hiza geri with lifted knee.
3. Tori steps and tries to push uke with morote shotei uchi. Tori ducks under and to the side (nanami, facing tori's back), kicking tori behind tori's knee driving tori to the ground. Uke may simulate pulling tori's head back and to the ground, gouging eyes.
4. Tori steps oi zuki chudan. Uke does hiki uke and pulls tori forward getting behind tori. Uke follows with a choke, taking tori to the ground.
5. Tori steps and attacks gyaku zuki jodan. Uke does a block on the same side. Uke turns into tori, blocks his hips, pulls down on the attacking arm, and throws tori to the ground, finishing with an arm break or eye gouge.

Ippon (Jiyu) Kumite Drills

1. All yakusoku ippon kumite drills but with no count.
2. All yakusoku ippon kumite drills but with one step.
3. First specify, then let tori attack with a head, chest, or down punch (first with a count, then without). Uke does any counter.
4. Specify just kicks.
5. Any technique (first with a count, then without).

Yakusoku Kumite

In yakusoku kumite, tori may do one or more attacks, and uke may do one or more blocks and counters, often ending with a takedown. Because both partners know what is expected Yakusoku kumite can be used to practice more deadly techniques. Creating different combinations can be fun. A good idea to focus on is ending each counter with an attack to the eyes, throat (choking) or groin. It is my understanding that this is how almost all counters ended in the early training days with Miyagi Chojun Sensei. Some yakusoku kumite drills are listed here.

Yakusoku Kumite Drills

1. Tori attacks mae geri, then gyaku zuki chudan. Uke blocks joge uke, then grabs tori's throat and groin. Uke squeezes and pulls groin, and grips and pushes throat, then steps through with a takedown (pulling belt instead of groin is okay in the dojo).
2. Tori attacks with a morote shotei uchi push, uke does morote chudan yoko uke, grabs tori's head with both hands and twists it to the ground.
3. Tori attacks tettsui uchi jodan. Uke cross blocks jodan, turns into the punch and to the side of tori while maintaining the grip on the punch (letting it slide a little in practice). The application is an arm break and throw.
4. Tori attacks with migi mae geri kekomi gedan. Uke blocks with hidarai gedan uke, keeping hold of the kicking leg (as in Saifa bunkai), then uke simultaneously steps in, places his foot behind tori's supporting leg and strikes migi shotei zuki, pushing tori to ground. Finish with a foot lock.
5. From hidarai han zenkutsu dachi, tori attacks mae geri off front leg and sets foot down in front. Uke sabakis (pivots) back, blocks gedan barai and then stomps on tori's front foot with his right foot and pins it to the ground. A migi haito zuki to the front of tori's neck will take him to the ground. End with arm break and eye gouge.

Jiyu Kumite

Jiyu kumite translates as, "free style kumite." This can be done by students and can successfully approximate a real fight scenario, especially if takedowns are used. Control, focus and technique are some of the goals in jiyu kumite.

In the Army, people are not given real ammunition and told to shoot at each other for practice. This type of kumite is meant to represent a street fight, but not be one. Dojo fighting is to be safe, with people taking care of each other.

Randori is light jiyu kumite. It is done slowly and softly. The more contact that is used, the more gear is needed. Gear including foam head and hand protection, and a cup is required for promotional exams. They are hot and awkward so they are not always used in the dojo if light contact is specified. However, it is a good idea to get used to them before an exam. I have found the following jiyu kumite drills to be useful.

Jiyu Kumite Drills

1. Only use one arm, then only use the next arm, then only one leg, then only the next leg.
2. Only hands.
3. Only feet.
4. Only left side.
5. Only right side.
6. One person against wall, blocking only.
7. Shiko dachi locking left leg (side to side) and sparring, then rotate.
8. Zenkutsu dachi locking forward leg and sparring, then rotate.
9. Focus shield between partners as a barrier, then remove.
10. Have everyone kumite each other by rotating partners.
11. One person spars with everyone who is in line by rank.
12. Use only techniques from Gekisai Dai Ichi (or another individual kata).
13. Use a standing Wavemaster as an obstacle between two people, much the same way as barrels are between rodeo clowns and bulls. If someone gets tired, they can hide behind the Wavemaster.
14. Dim lights and play loud music.
15. Briefly, turn the lights off.
16. Outside on various terrains.
17. Focus shields on the floor as obstacles.
18. Uke walks between two tori. Sensei points out which tori will attack but uke doesn't know (sometimes both attack).

Iri Kumi (Hard Jiyu)

Iri kumi is meant to test how much you can take as well as how much you can give (give and take as in a punishment sort of way). Some styles wear shin pads but others do not. All wear a mouthpiece, foam head, hand, footgear and cup. Women must use chest protectors.

I feel a student should do iri kumi at least once in order to test him or herself; however, it is understandable why some may never do this. Injuries can occur easily and iri kumi must not be taken lightly. Always have a first aid kit handy.

Grabbing, kneeing, leg whipping, sweeping, hard contact to the body and controlled throws are allowed. If caged headgear is used, contact to the face is allowed. Using caged headgear takes practice and it should be worn during dojo training to get familiar with it before an event. Because throws are permitted, iri kumi is often done on floor mats. Matches include two one-minute rounds with a thirty-second rest. A majority decision by judges indicates the winner.

It is important to note that students do not have to participate in kumite. If a student feels uncomfortable, and the sensei insists on that student doing kumite, then the sensei may be liable if the student is injured. It is better to be safe than sorry. Safety gear for the head, mouth, hands, groin, and feet can be used as the intensity of contact in kumite increases. Gear is mandatory for iri kumi.

Illegal Techniques

The following is a list of many illegal techniques in tournaments and the techniques are prohibited in the dojo as well. It is not a definitive list. Always abide by it and any other instructions given by the person in charge.

Illegal Techniques

1. An uncontrolled throw.
2. An upward hand technique to the face
4. Any open hand technique to the face.
5. A face technique with excessive follow through.
6. Any technique causing unconsciousness is considered to be excessive.
7. Putting one's self in a defenseless position.
8. Any throw originating with the opponents head and/or wrist.
8. Any throw that involves a wrist/arm/leg lock or choke shall be illegal.
9. Any throw whereby the opponent is thrown to the ground with the thrower's weight landing on them.
10. Any throw that results in the opponent's inability to land safely.
11. All biting, gouging, finger twisting and pressure point manipulation.
12 Any face contact is prohibited below brown belt.
13. Any malicious and/or repeated attacks to the arms, legs or joints.
14. Hair pulling.
15. Biting.

Liability and Treatment

Waivers are a part of everyday life. Polo lessons require a stack of waivers to be signed, as do simple swimming lessons. It is important that every student, or their parent/guardian sign *Release from Liability* and *Hold Harmless Agreement* before participation in karate and kobudo. This especially needs to be done before any kumite is attempted (see Figure 8.1).

It is important to note that students do not have to participate in kumite or other training if they do not wish to. If a student objects, and the Sensei insists on that student doing training like kumite, then the Sensei may be liable if the student is injured. It is better to be safe than sorry.

It is also important to stress during training the proper use of karate as self defense or defense of others. Talk about "reasonable force." Not only is this a good practice for ethical reasons, it can protect you against vicarious liability as well.

It is very important for children under 18 years old to have a *Medical and Emergency Authorization: Consent to Treat Form* on file. This comes from my experience as a teacher in the public sector. It is more likely that this might be needed in the event there is an earthquake, or some other natural disaster, than a student needing it for something that happens in the dojo. I believe parents would be very appreciative if you ask for this information. Figure 8.2 is an example of a *Medical and Emergency Authorization: Consent to Treat Form*.

Release from Liability

RELEASE FROM LIABILITY
AND HOLD HARMLESS AGREEMENT

By signing this *Release from Liability Hold and Harmless Agreement*, I am stating that I have read it in its entirety and fully understand that training in karate and kobudo are physical activities where injury or accidental death can occur. Fully understanding the risk involved, I choose to participate, and as such, I release from liability and hold harmless Michael P. Cogan, assistant instructors, guest instructors, and all other participants from any and all liability that may occur as a result of my participation. I waive any and all claims or cause of action.

I also understand that no medical, health, or life insurance of any kind is implied or provided and that I am fully responsible for any and all costs that may be incurred as a result of injury or illness due to my participation in karate and kobudo.

By signing, I am also making testimony that I am of sound mind and body and that I do not suffer from any physical or mental conditions that may affect my participation in karate and kobudo.

I promise never to use what is taught to me to harm another unjustifiably. I shall obey the commands of the instructors at all times, unless I feel in imminent danger. By teaching these techniques, the instructors in no way acknowledge the competency level of any participant and are hereby released from liability and held harmless from any and all vicarious liability.

_____

(Participant Signature and Parent/Guardian if Participant is under 18)
(Date)

Print Name _____
Address _____
Phone Number _____
Birth Date (Confidential) _____
Previous Training, Instructors and Current Rank _____

_____

Figure 8.1

Consent to Treat

MEDICAL AND EMERGENCY AUTHORIZATION: CONSENT TO TREAT FORM

Student Name _____

Social Security Number _____

Birth Date _____

Address _____

Phone _____

In the event of an accident, injury, or illness we can be reached by calling:

Name _____

Address _____

Phone _____

If we cannot be reached, please call one of the following persons who will take responsibility for the student's care. We authorize the release of the student to these persons in the event of a disaster:

Name _____

Address _____

Phone _____

If emergency treatment by a doctor or an ambulance is needed and we cannot be reached, we authorize the school to call our family physician or health advisor:

Name _____

Address _____

Phone _____

We understand that the school assumes no financial responsibility for medical care or ambulance cost:

Date _____

Parent/Guardian Signature _____

Additional Information

Does this child have (or has he/she had) any illnesses, injuries, or allergies (especially to medications), which are important to know about?

_____

_____

_____

Figure 8.2

Kumite

Chapter 9

Kids' Stuff

Chapter 9 Table of Contents

Kids' Stuff

Introduction

Fortunately, kids can do almost all the things adults can do with few exceptions. Almost all of the information in the other chapters of this manual can be done with kids. Some guidelines and ideas with special attention to character education are provided here.

This being said, there are a few things that children should not do. Sanchin is not done with kids. Kotei ate is not done either. Makiwara training is out. Adult bones have finished growing and need increase bone and fascia density which kotei ate provides. Children's bones grow from the growth plate at the ends of the bones. If these growth plates are damaged, irregular growth patterns can occur. Children are not permitted to do iri kumi. Soft focus shields are recommended.

Classes for children are shorter than for adults. A common range is between 45 minutes and an hour. As with adults hydration is important. There is the potential for students to run into each other. Be safe and give clear instructions.

Mini ranks can be given in between formal ranks. Mini exams can be similar to regular exams only smaller. The emphasis for a mini exam may focus on only one thing. The mini exams should focus on improvement and without pass/fail pressure. The students can earn an extra colored stripe on their belts for each mini exam. Each color stripe can represent a different skill such as red for kihon, white for kata and blue for kumite. These mini exams can be made a requirement before each promotion. Having the extra stripes be red, white and blue can help promote patriotism. So, can beginning each class with the Pledge of Allegiance. Mini Mees (helpers) can help the Sensei by doing junbi undo next to the Sensei.

Police can be recruited to speak to the children (and adults). They can talk about different topics such as reasonable force and how to report a crime. Fire personnel can also be contacted to discuss fire prevention and safety. Older students can learn first aid and CPR. Each child must have a signed Consent to Treat Form. This is found in Chapter 8 under liability.

Character Education and Student Safety

Character Education

According to oral tradition, the founder of Goju Ryu, Chojun Miyagi Sensei took the whole person into account when training. In *The History of Karate* (Higaonna, 1995) states,

> "Miyagi did not just educate his students in technique only, but also concerned himself with the development of the human spirit. It was his wish that through the practice and study of Okinawan Karate people would become better human beings. After training, Miyagi talked about the importance of diet for Karate practitioners. He also lectured on subjects as diverse as the spirit of a *bujin* (martial artist), the correct path for human beings, principles of right living and the importance of martial arts *shinzui* (truth) in the formation of the human character."

The Kogen Kan Mission Statement bears repeating here.

The Kogen Kan Mission Statement

The Kogen Kan is a traditional school that strives to provide students with safe, professional, world-class instruction on the history, techniques and virtues of Okinawan Goju Ryu Karatedo and Matayoshi Kobudo. While developing a strong mind, body and indomitable spirit, students learn to be self-disciplined, respectful, kind and honest.

I believe this Mission Statement is in keeping with what Miyagi Sensei was trying to achieve. The Kogen Kan is registered with the Jefferson Center for Character Education. I have used some of their materials at my public school site. I am happy to report it has been adapted to fit a martial arts curriculum. This curriculum is called, "Be a S.T.A.R. in the Martial Arts." The Jefferson Center interprets the STAR acronym as, "Success Through Accepting Responsibility." Students develop being responsible by setting and achieving goals. Accepting personal responsibility improves attendance, punctuality and reliability. Another Jefferson Center interpretation for the STAR acronym is, "Stop, and Think, Act and Review."

Character education is of paramount importance when working with youth. The Kogen Kan stresses many other virtues not mentioned above, including courage, justice, integrity, caring and politeness. These values stretch across cultural and religious lines. When students develop these attributes, they improve their self-confidence, self-esteem, and they gain a positive attitude.

These virtues are reinforced when discussing self-defense. We teach students to avoid conflict. This is often done at the "stop and think" stage. If a conflict is unavoidable then only reasonable force is acceptable. Sometimes this is only simple verbal interaction such and yelling, "No!" or "Stop!" Hopefully, physical force will not be necessary, but if it is, students are taught to only use enough to escape safely. Protection of yourself and others does not include loosing control and hurting a perpetrator beyond what is needed to resolve the situation. Reviewing any incident is a learning experience. If a student has an altercation, the student is required to report it. The incident is reviewed with a focus on problem solving and finding new solutions for the future.

<u>Student Safety</u>

The Kogen Kan looks at student safety using tools from Safety Kids Inc. http://www.safetykids.org/index.html . Two pages from this web site are included here with permission. These web pages list Safety "Check" Points For Kids and Safety "Check" Points For Parents. The Kogen Kan also uses tools from the National Center for Missing and Exploited Children http://www.missingkids.com/ . This center publishes many materials on child safety including child identification, how to travel safely and cyber safety. This center is associated with the International Center for Missing and Exploited Children. These tools increase awareness and help children be safe and secure. Having a sense of safety is one of the primary needs children must have met before any learning can take place.

Safety "Check" Points for Kids

1. Most of the people in the world are good and helpful!

2. **CHECK FIRST** before you go <u>anywhere</u>, with <u>anyone</u>, for <u>any</u> reason at <u>any</u> time!! Check with whoever is in charge of you at the time.

3. Adults can get help from other adults. You do not need to help anyone find a lost puppy, unload a truck, etc., without checking first.

4. Know your full name, address (including state), and telephone number with the area code. Know your parents' names, too.

5. If you are separated in a store, FREEZE and YELL! Stay where you are and yell your parents first and last name. Ask a clerk or a mother with children for help.

6. If anyone tries to move or hurt you, make sure you scream, kick, fight, and yell, "You're not my dad (or mom)!"

7. Use the buddy system; go in groups.

8. You are in charge of your body. No one has the right to touch you in a way that makes you feel uncomfortable. If you are told to keep it a secret, make sure you tell an adult you trust.

9. When you are home alone, keep the door locked and closed for everyone. Let the phone ring, let the answering machine pick it up, or work out a system with your parents so that no one realizes you are home alone.

10. When you are on the Internet, keep personal information to yourself! Ask your parent what sites you can visit and what information you can give out.

Make good choices and wise decisions!
Follow these "check" points and you'll stay safe!

Copyright and TM by Safety Kids, Inc.
P.O. Box 27120
Pittsburgh, Pa 15235
Phone: (412)371-7171 Fax: (412)241-2535
Permission is given to reproduce this page provided that <u>NO</u> changes are
made.

Safety "Check" Points for Parents

1. Tell your children that you will love them *unconditionally* no matter what happens. You may not like their actions or words, but you still love them.

2. Teach your children safety tips in small, repeated doses. Avoid using the word "stranger"! Children think they know people more than they actually do, and the term stranger is ineffective. Remind them always to CHECK FIRST before going any where with any one.

3. Get in the habit of using the phrase, "It is OK because I am with you" before giving permission to take candy, money, etc. from anyone, or to speak to someone unknown. Children then learn that they can not do these things if you are not with them. This technique works!

4. Never ever leave a child unattended in a vehicle. It can take three seconds for someone to steal the car. You are also subject to a fine!

5. Give your young child the names of two safety persons who can always be trusted. Use a code word with children older than third grade.

6. Monitor what your children are doing on the computer. Instruct them never to give out personal information on the internet. Make sure you and your children know how to be "cyber-safe".

7. Have your child wear items with their names on them inside the house. Children are more likely to trust someone who calls them by name.

8. Remind your children that they are in charge of their bodies and no one has the right to touch them in a way to make them feel uncomfortable.

9. LISTEN if your child tells you that he/she does not want to be with someone. Find out why and respect that feeling. Open the lines of communication.

10. Update photos four times a year for preschoolers and once a year after that. Keep an up-to-date record with important data bout your child.

Kids' Karate Activities

1. Hop on one foot across floor. Then hop with both feet low to floor, forward and backward.

2. Army crawl keeping butt down, moving on forearms and toes.

3. Jump rope.

4. Throwing a headgear to the students while they are in line and telling them to punch, kick or both.

5. Wheelbarrow races.

6. Wheelbarrow races with pushups.

7. Kihon can be done on the heavy bag to develop balance.

8. Crab walks (face the ceiling on all fours, butt off ground).

9. Supermen (squat, then leap as high and far as you can extending your arms).

10. Kick with cups of water in hands without spilling (keeps hands up).

11. Inch worm push-ups (push-up, walk feet to hands, release and fall forward, repeat).

12. Sensei Says, basically with emphasis on right and left hand recognition. (English and Japanese).

13. Kids can kick the heavy bag while it is resting on the floor with an adult holding it up vertically (that way it is low enough).

14. Kick, punch or block races. How many in a short time.

15. Follow the sensei while running.

16. Leap Frog (with kicks and punches).

17. Grab and Run aka Ro Shambo. Sensei tries to grab a student as they walk by. If they get away, sensei can pursue. If they are caught, they need to kick, punch and escape. Sensei can be in seiza to even the playing field.

18. Slap hand reaction drill.

Kids' Karate Activities

19. Duck Walks.

20. Bear Walks. All four facing down.

21. Crab Walks. All fours facing up.

22. Scarf or paper punch or kick.

23. Step techniques. Have the kids step up on a platform and do a technique, then step back down (like step aerobics).

24. Various games can be done with hoola-hoops. One is to step inside and do a technique, then step out.

25. One mile run. Timed. For older kids and adults.

26.　　a) Place 2 parallel lines on the floor, about 2 feet long, and about 6 inches apart.

b) Place 2 participants on the lines, facing each other, with toes touching a line, in say heiko dachi, as such:

V　　V

_____

_____

^　　^

c) Have each person place their palms against each other (i.e., patty-cakes style...).

d) Have the participants push each other's palms, alternating as necessary between push and relax / absorb.

e) Loser is the person that loses his / her balance, either forward or backward, and having to move their feet to stay upright.

f) Key point: No hooking of the other person's hand with the thumbs!

27. Kick, hit and yell. This is an anti-abduction drill. Yelling words such as "No!", "Help!", "Fire!" and "You're not my mother/father!".

28. Red Light Green Light while doing oi zuki, gyaku zuki, mae geri etc.

The Pledge of Allegiance

I pledge allegiance

to the flag

of the United States of America

and to the Republic

for which it stands:

one Nation

under God,

indivisible,

with liberty and justice for all.

When reciting the pledge of allegiance, civilians should stand at attention or with the right hand over the heart. Males should remove their hats. Armed services personnel in uniform should face the flag and give the military salute.

Kids' Stuff

Notes

Chapter 10

Items for Framing

Chapter 10 Table of Contents

Introduction

In many Goju Ryu dojo you will often find three pictures. They are of Bodhidharma, Higaonna Kanryo Sensei and Chojun Miyagi Sensei. These pictures are provided here and may be reproduced for personal use.

Bodhidharma (also known as Daruma) is a Buddhist monk, who came to China from India around 475 A.D. He is considered by many to be the patriarch of the martial arts in China, and from there, Japan and Okinawa.

Higaonna Kanryo Sensei (also known as Higashiona Kanryo Sensei) brought back many kata from China to Okinawa. He established and taught Naha Te. It was with his instruction that Chojun Miyagi Sensei became proficient at karate.

Chojun Miyagi Sensei systematized the instruction of Higaonna Kanryo Sensei into the style of Goju Ryu. He developed Junbi undo as a way to warm up and protect the body from injury. He taught many students who have spread his art worldwide.

Also included is a certificate of rank and Seishin Award. These are provided to illustrate some of the criteria for successful advancement and meritorious conduct. Character and conduct are equally as important as knowledge and abilities. Effort given toward learning is always recognized.

The maps of Okinawa and Japan are courtesy of The Central Intelligence Agency (CIA), 1990 and 2002 respectively. As such, it is public domain and can be copied freely.

Bodhidharma

Kanryo Higaonna Sensei

Miyagi Chojun Sensei

Chapter 10: Items for Framing

*Kanryo Higaonna Sensei
Founder of Naha Te*

*Miyagi Chojun Sensei
Founder of Goju Ryu*

This certifies that, through studious and diligent practice,

Dan Tappe

~~~~~~

has consistently exhibited the <u>character</u> and <u>conduct</u> befitting a student of Okinawan Goju Ryu Karatedo and successfully demonstrated the <u>knowledge</u> and <u>abilities</u> commensurate with the rank of

San Kyu

~~~~~~

As rank increases so does responsibility. The recipient of this rank is expected to uphold the virtues of Goju Ryu Karatedo. These virtues may be shown by way of continued research, continued practice and continued assistance of others.

The Kogen Kan hereby bestows this rank.

/   /

~~~~~~

*Michael P. Cogan, MSE and Nidan in Okinawan Goju Ryu Karatedo;
Chief Instructor of the Kogen Kan*

Chapter 10: Items for Framing

The Kogen Kan Seishin Award

This Seishin Award is given to persons exhibiting meritorious conduct.
This conduct includes, but is not limited to: enthusiasm, participation, determination, honesty and effort in learning,

This Kogen Kan Seishin Award is gratefully given to

_____

On this day: _____

Signed: _____
Michael P. Cogan, MSE Chief Instructor of the Kogen Kan

Map of Okinawa

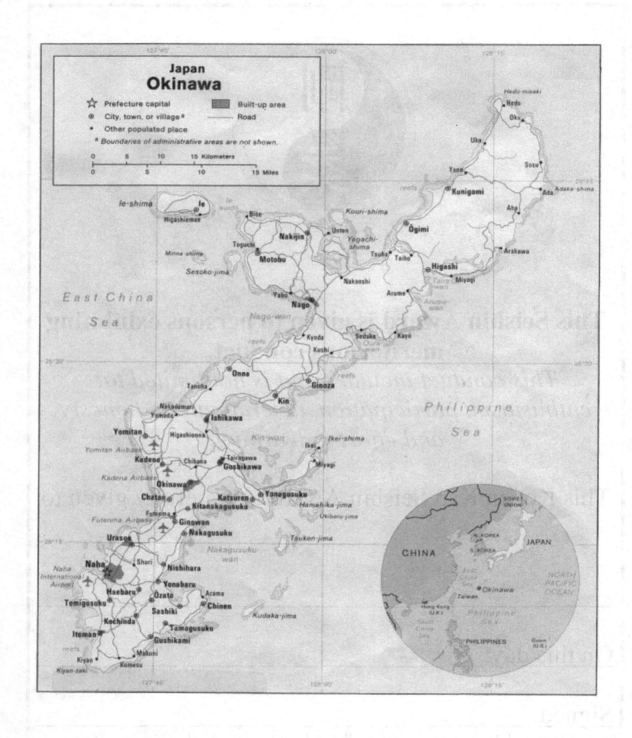

Map of Japan

Chapter 10: Items for Framing

Items for Framing

<u>Notes</u>

Appendix A: Ukemi

Who hasn't had a fear of falling? Without reviewing the literature of scientific studies, I can pretty much guess that falling is around the top three phobias. I can let my turtle roam freely on my deck because I know he will stay away from the edge. Even he is smart enough to know falling can be bad. One way to capture elephants is to dig a moat about three feet deep. Then put a bridge across it and sugar cane on the island. When the elephants cross the bridge to eat the sugar cane, pull the bridge away. The elephants will be trapped because they won't step father than their trunks will naturally reach. They are smart enough to know falling can be bad.

Okay. Turtles, elephants and humans all agree falling can be bad, but can it be safe? Look around. We fall all the time. Think about when you first learned to ride a bike. Did you fall? Probably. Did you get up and try again? Probably. Skier, skateboarders and football players will all say falling is part of the game. So to is it in karate.

In karate, we have the benefit of practicing falling. Ukemi is the practice of falling. One needs to be proficient at fall so as not to be injured while practicing. Fortunately, there are only four main falls to practice.

They are:

1. **The Roll**: Tuck in the chin, reach around as if holing a beach ball with your arms and roll from the shoulder, down the back and possibly end up on the feet.

2. **The Fall to the Side**: Tuck in the chin, breath out while falling, spread out the weight out over the side of the body and slap the ground with the arm at a 45° angle out to the side of the body.

3. **The Fall to the Front**: Tuck in the chin, breath out while falling, land on the forearms with the elbows tucked in to the side of the body.

4. **The Fall to the Back**: Tuck in the chin, breath out while falling, land with both the arms at a 45° angle while dispersing the weight over the body.

I am including these falls in this appendix because they can be practiced individually without partners. I recommend a "crash mat" and tumbling mats be available. First practice at low-level positions then gradually move higher. Practice both sides while rolling and falling to the side. Initially start in a stationary position then add movement, slowly building up speed. Later, you can have a partner throw you and progress through the steps discussed above. Throwing is not discussed in this guidebook except to say that each bunkai can be adapted to include a throw to the ground and a finishing technique.

A Goju Ryu Guidebook:
The Kogen Kan Manual for Karate

Appendix B: Kyusho

It is thought that a vital energy called "chi" (Chinese) or "ki" (Japanese) travels through pathways called "meridians." These meridians are called the Lung, Large Intestine, Stomach, Spleen, Heart, Small Intestine, Bladder, Kidney, Pericardium, Triple Warmer, Gallbladder and Liver. Each meridian helps regulate the function of different muscles, organs and even moods of the body. The energy usually takes a 24-hour cycle through the meridians spending approximately two hours in each beginning with the lung at 3:00 am. to 5:00 am. And following the order listed above.

Along these meridians are Kyusho or pressure points. Pressure points are areas that when struck, pressed or manipulated have a profound effect on the receiving individual. This effect can be both good and bad. These point work accumulatively. If several points are activated at the same time the effect is geometric. It is more than the sum of the parts.

The names of pressure points can be different depending on what course of study is followed. There are Japanese names, Okinawan and Chinese names. Still others use numbers and initials of the meridians to describe location. The twelfth point on the Gall Balder meridian would be GB-12. The different names can make discussions and study difficult. What is presented here are some pressure points with Japanese names and English gross anatomical descriptions. They are also broken down into there general locations of head and neck, arms, torso and legs.

Two rules of thumbs about many pressure points are: 1. they are often found on the shaded regions of the body and 2. they are generally the size of the eye. For example, below the nose would be shaded from light if it were shone from above. If the area (about the size of the eye) is activated it can cause tearing and will bleed profusely if the integrity of the circulatory system is breached there. Two terms often heard while studying pressure points are: 1. Sealing the Breath and 2. Sealing the blood. The first term refers to striking the larynx or the diaphragm in such a way as it at least stops the opponent form breathing temporarily. The second term refers to striking the circulatory system so that the brain dose not have blood flow.

The students will be asked do show the location of each pressure point and how it might be manipulate for an exam. Each pressure point is worth two points and 90% is passing. Please try to visualize these pressure points while practicing kata and kihon. People are often told to visualize an opponent while practicing but I believe this should be taken one step further and pressure points must be visualized as well.

Appendix B: Kyusho

Head and Neck
1. **Tendo** (Crown of the Head)
2. **Tento** (Area between Crown and Forehead)
3. **Komekami** (Temple)
4. **Mimi** (Ears)
5. **Miken** (Bridge of the Nose)
6. **Seidon** (Area Above and Below the Eyes)
7. **Gansei** (Eyeballs)
8. **Jinchu** (Region Below the Nose)
9. **Gekon** (Below Lower Lip)
10. **Mikazuki** (Jaw)
11. **Dokko** (Behind the Ears)
12. **Keichu** (Nape of Neck)
13. **Shofu** (Side of Neck)
14. **Sonu** (Base of Throat, Between Throat and Sternum)
15. **Hichu** (Adam's Apple, Larynx)

Chest and Back
1. **Danchu** (Sternum)
2. **Kyototsu** (Base of Sternum)
3. **Suigetsu** (Solar-Plexus)
4. **Kyoei** (Below the Armpits, between the 5th and 6th ribs)
5. **Ganchu** (Below the Nipples)
6. **Denko** (Between 7th and 8th Ribs)
7. **Inazuma** (Side of body, Above Hips)
8. **Myojo** (Below Navel)
9. **Soda** (Between Shoulder Blades)
10. **Katsusatsu** (Middle of spine, Between 5th and 6th Vertebra)
11. **Jinzo** (Kidney)
12. **Kabzo** (Liver)

13. **Kodenko** (Base of Spine)
14. **Bitei** (Coccyx)

Arm
1. **Wanshun** (Tricep)
2. **Hijizume** (Elbow Joint)
3. **Udekansetsu** (Arm Joint)
4. **Kote** (Wrist)
5. **Uchijakuzawa**/Miyakudokoro (Inside Forearm at Pulse)
6. **Sotojakuzawa** (Wrist Edge Above Pulse)
7. **Shuko** (Back of the Hand)
8. **Yubi** (Fingers)

Legs
1. **Kinteki** (Testicles)
2. **Yako** (Inside Upper Thigh)
3. **Fukuto** (Outside Lower Thigh)
4. **Hizakansetsu** (Knee Joint)
5. **Ushirohizakansetsu** (Behind Knee Joint)
6. **Kokotsu** (Inside Shin)
7. **Uchikurobushi** (Inside Ankle Joint)
8. **Kori** (Instep)
9. **Kusagakure** (Outside Top Edge of Foot)
10. **Ushiro-Inazuma** (Below Buttocks)
11. **Sobi** (Base of Calf)
12. **Akiresuken** (Achilles tendon)
13. **Ashinoyubi** (toes)

Appendix C: Basic Facts of Okinawa

These basic facts regarding Okinawa and Japan are being provided so that students can understand some entry-level information about the prefecture Okinawa and the country of Japan.

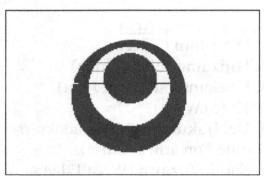

Okinawa Prefecture's Flag Description

The flag is white with a red circle inside a larger red circle. The inner circle represents Okinawa. The white around it represents "peace." The outer circle represents the ocean. It became the Okinawa Prefecture's flag in 1992.

Okinawa Prefecture's Tree: *Ryukyu Matsu* **(Ryukyu Pine)**
Pinus Luchuensis Mayr

A Ryukyu Pine is very prolific. It is used in bonsai, windbreaks, and planted along roadsides. It can reach a height of fifty feet. As the tree ages the tree crowns spread into gracefully shaped branches.

Okinawa Prefecture's Flower: *Deigo* **(Indian coral bean)** *Erythrina Orientalis Murray*

The Deigo tree is originally from India. Between March and May, the bright red flowers bloom in clusters along the length of the branches. It is used in making traditional Ryukyuan lacquer ware. It became the flower of the Okinawa Prefecture in 1972.

Okinawa Prefecture's Bird: Okinawan Woodpecker (Pryers' woodpecker or noguchi gera)
Sapheopipo Noguchii (Seebohm)

This species of exists exclusively in the northern part of Okinawa. It has been designated as a natural treasure of Japan.

Appendix C: Basic Facts of Okinawa

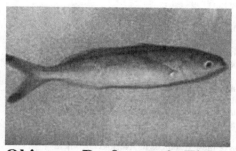

Okinawa Prefecture's Fish: Banana Fish (*Takasago*, locally known as *Gurukun*)

Caesio diagramma

This fish is silver with a bright gold streak running horizontally across the length of both sides. The Okinawan people traditionally caught this fish by driving it into nets. It is used for fish cakes (kamaboko) and often served in local homes.

Poem by: Seiko Miyasato
Composed by: Shigeru Shiroma

1. The day breaks over the clean ocean
Clouds are cleared over the peaceful islands
Dawn bell sounds throughout the world
We now face the glorious morning
Gone are the days of trials
Oh! We solemnly swear
We swear eternal peace on Okinawa

2. The Black Current runs around the islands
Green mountains and rivers glowing
We, the fellow citizens are stirred up
To build a new, independent and prosperous Okinawa
Now, let us build eternal peace
On our home islands

3. The skies are filled with lights
Stain the Deigo flowers with brilliant color
The folk culture inherited for generations
Now brilliantly shines over our home islands
Let us create our own culture
For future Okinawa

Information and pictures courtesy of Okinawahttp://www.pref.okinawa.jp/symbol/index-e.html retrieved 1-7-2003

Appendix D: Basic Facts of Japan

Japanese' Flag Description
The flag is white with a large red disk in the center (representing the sun without rays).

Japan

Background:
While retaining its time-honored culture, Japan rapidly absorbed Western technology during the late 19th and early 20th centuries. After its devastating defeat in World War II, Japan recovered to become the second most powerful economy in the world and a staunch ally of the US. While the emperor retains his throne as a symbol of national unity, actual power rests in networks of powerful politicians, bureaucrats, and business executives. The economy experienced a major slowdown in the 1990s following three decades of unprecedented growth.

Geography Japan

Location: Eastern Asia, island chain between the North Pacific Ocean and the Sea of Japan, east of the Korean Peninsula

Geographic coordinates:
36 00 N, 138 00 E

Map references:
Asia

Area:
total: 377,835 sq km
note: includes Bonin Islands (Ogasawara-gunto), Daito-shoto, Minami-jima, Okino-tori-shima, Ryukyu Islands (Nansei-shoto), and Volcano Islands (Kazan-retto)
water: 3,091 sq km
land: 374,744 sq km

Area - comparative:
slightly smaller than California

Land boundaries:
0 km

Coastline:
29,751 km

Climate:
varies from tropical in south to cool temperate in north

Terrain:
mostly rugged and mountainous

Elevation extremes:
lowest point: Hachiro-gata -4 m
highest point: Fujiyama 3,776 m

Natural resources:
negligible mineral resources, fish

Land use:
arable land: 12%
permanent crops: 1%
other: 87% (1998 est.)

Irrigated land:
26,790 sq km (1998 est.)

Natural hazards:
many dormant and some active volcanoes; about 1,500 seismic occurrences (mostly tremors) every year; tsunamis; typhoons

Environment - current issues:
air pollution from power plant emissions results in acid rain; acidification of lakes and reservoirs degrading water quality and threatening aquatic life; Japan is one of the largest consumers of fish and tropical timber, contributing to the depletion of these resources in Asia and elsewhere

Environment - international agreements:
party to: Antarctic-Environmental Protocol, Antarctic-Marine Living Resources, Antarctic Seals, Antarctic Treaty, Biodiversity, Climate Change, Desertification, Endangered Species, Environmental Modification, Hazardous Wastes, Law of the Sea, Marine Dumping, Nuclear Test Ban, Ozone Layer Protection, Ship Pollution, Tropical Timber 83, Tropical Timber 94, Wetlands, Whaling
signed, but not ratified: Climate Change-Kyoto Protocol

Geography - note:
strategic location in northeast Asia

People Japan

Population:
126,974,628 (July 2002 est.)

Age structure:
0-14 years: 14.5% (male 9,465,282; female 8,999,888)
15-64 years: 67.5% (male 43,027,320; female 42,586,112)
65 years and over: 18% (male 9,664,112; female 13,231,914) (2002 est.)

Life expectancy at birth:
total population: 80.91 years
female: 84.25 years (2002 est.)
male: 77.73 years

Nationality:
noun: Japanese (singular and plural)
adjective: Japanese

Ethnic groups:
Japanese 99%, others 1% (Korean 51,126, Chinese 24,424, Brazilian 18,223, Filipino 8,995, other 23,792) (2000)

Religions:
observe both Shinto and Buddhist 84%, other 16% (including Christian 0.7%)

Languages:
Japanese

Literacy:
definition: age 15 and over can read and write
total population: 99% (1970 est.)
male: NA%
female: NA%

Government Japan

Country name:
conventional long form: none
conventional short form: Japan

A Goju Ryu Guidebook:
The Kogen Kan Manual for Karate

Appendix D: Basic Facts of Japan

Government type:
constitutional monarchy with a parliamentary government

Capital:
Tokyo

Administrative divisions:
47 prefectures; Aichi, Akita, Aomori, Chiba, Ehime, Fukui, Fukuoka, Fukushima, Gifu, Gumma, Hiroshima, Hokkaido, Hyogo, Ibaraki, Ishikawa, Iwate, Kagawa, Kagoshima, Kanagawa, Kochi, Kumamoto, Kyoto, Mie, Miyagi, Miyazaki, Nagano, Nagasaki, Nara, Niigata, Oita, Okayama, Okinawa, Osaka, Saga, Saitama, Shiga, Shimane, Shizuoka, Tochigi, Tokushima, Tokyo, Tottori, Toyama, Wakayama, Yamagata, Yamaguchi, Yamanashi

Independence:
660 BC (traditional founding by Emperor Jimmu)

National holiday:
Birthday of Emperor AKIHITO, 23 December (1933)

Constitution:
3 May 1947

Diplomatic representation in the US:
chief of mission: Ambassador Ryozo KATO
FAX: [1] (202) 328-2187
consulate(s): Saipan (Northern Mariana Islands)
consulate(s) general: Anchorage, Atlanta, Boston, Chicago, Denver, Detroit, Hagatna (Guam), Honolulu, Houston, Kansas City (Missouri), Los Angeles, Miami, New Orleans, New York, Portland (Oregon), San Francisco, and Seattle
chancery: 2520 Massachusetts Avenue NW, Washington, DC 20008
telephone: [1] (202) 238-6700

Diplomatic representation from the US:
chief of mission: Ambassador Howard H. BAKER, Jr.
embassy: 1-10-5 Akasaka, Minato-ku, Tokyo 107-8420
mailing address: Unit 45004, Box 205, APO AP 96337-5004
telephone: [81] (03) 3224-5000
FAX: [81] (03) 3505-1862
consulate(s) general: Naha (Okinawa), Osaka-Kobe, Sapporo
consulate(s): Fukuoka, Nagoya

Flag description:
white with a large red disk (representing the sun without rays) in the center

Economy Japan

Economy - overview:
Government-industry cooperation, a strong work ethic, mastery of high technology, and a comparatively small defense allocation (1% of GDP) have helped Japan advance with extraordinary rapidity to the rank of second most technologically powerful economy in the world after the US and third largest economy in the world after the US and China. One notable characteristic of the economy is the working together of manufacturers, suppliers, and distributors in closely-knit groups called keiretsu. A second basic feature has been the guarantee of lifetime employment for a substantial portion of the urban labor force. Both features are now eroding. Industry, the most important sector of the economy, is heavily dependent on imported raw materials and fuels. The much smaller agricultural sector is highly subsidized and protected, with crop yields among the highest in the world. Usually self-sufficient in rice, Japan must import about 50% of its requirements of other grain and fodder crops. Japan maintains one of the world's largest fishing fleets and accounts for nearly 15% of the global catch. For three decades overall real economic growth had been spectacular: a 10% average in the 1960s, a 5% average in the 1970s, and a 4% average in the 1980s. Growth slowed markedly in the 1990s largely because of the aftereffects of overinvestment during the late 1980s and contractionary domestic policies intended to wring speculative excesses from the stock and real estate markets. Government efforts to revive economic growth have met with little success and were further hampered in 2000-01 by the slowing of the US and Asian economies. The crowding of habitable land area and the aging of the population are two major long-run problems. Robotics constitutes a key long-term economic strength, with Japan possessing 410,000 of the world's 720,000 "working robots".

GDP:
purchasing power parity - $3.45 trillion (2001 est.)

GDP - real growth rate:
-0.3% (2001 est.)

GDP - per capita:
purchasing power parity - $27,200 (2001 est.)

GDP - composition by sector:
agriculture: 2%
industry: 36%
services: 62% (2000 est.)

Population below poverty line:
NA%

Household income or consumption by percentage share:
lowest 10%: 4.8%
highest 10%: 21.7% (1993)

Distribution of family income - Gini index:
24.9 (1993)

Inflation rate (consumer prices):
-0.6% (2001 est.)

Labor force:
67.7 million (December 2000)

Labor force - by occupation:
services 65%, industry 30%, agriculture 5%

Unemployment rate:
4.9% (2001)

Budget:
revenues: $441 billion
expenditures: $718 billion, including capital expenditures (public works only) of about $84 billion (FY01/02 est.)

Industries:
among world's largest and technologically advanced producers of motor vehicles, electronic equipment, machine tools, steel and nonferrous metals, ships, chemicals; textiles, processed foods

Industrial production growth rate:
-8.3% (2001 est.)

Electricity - production:
1.015 trillion kWh (2000)

Appendix D: Basic Facts of Japan

Electricity - production by source:
fossil fuel: 60.69%
hydro: 8.54%
other: 1.82% (2000)
nuclear: 28.95%

Electricity - consumption:
943.71 billion kWh (2000)

Electricity - exports:
0 kWh (2000)

Electricity - imports:
0 kWh (2000)

Agriculture - products:
rice, sugar beets, vegetables, fruit; pork, poultry, dairy
products, eggs; fish

Exports:
$404.6 billion (f.o.b., 2001 est.)

Exports - commodities:
motor vehicles, semiconductors, office machinery, chemicals

Exports - partners:
US 29.7%, Taiwan 7.5%, South Korea 6.4%, China 6.3%,
Hong Kong 5.7% (2000 est.)

Imports:
$331.6 billion (f.o.b., 2001 est.)

Imports - commodities:
fuels, foodstuffs, chemicals, textiles, office machinery

Imports - partners:
US 19%, China 14.5%, South Korea 5.4%, Taiwan 4.7%,
Indonesia 4.3%, Australia 3.9% (2000 est.)

Debt - external:
$NA

Economic aid - donor:
ODA, $9.1 billion (1999)

Currency:
yen (JPY)

Currency code:
JPY

Exchange rates:
yen per US dollar - 132.66 (January 2002), 121.53 (2001),
107.77 (2000), 113.91 (1999), 130.91 (1998),

Fiscal year:
1 April - 31 March

Military Japan

Military branches:
Japan Ground Self-Defense Force (Army), Japan Maritime
Self-Defense Force (Navy), Japan Air Self-Defense Force
(Air Force), Japanese Coast Guard

Military manpower - military age:
18 years of age (2002 est.)

Military manpower - availability:

males age 15-49: 29,644,498 (2002 est.)

Military manpower - fit for military service:
males age 15-49: 25,637,387 (2002 est.)

Military manpower - reaching military age annually:
males: 765,817 (2002 est.)

Military expenditures - dollar figure:
$40,774,300,000 (FY01)

Military expenditures - percent of GDP:
1% (FY01)

Transnational Issues Japan

Disputes - international:
islands of Etorofu, Kunashiri, and Shikotan, and the Habomai
group occupied by the Soviet Union in 1945, now
administered by Russia, claimed by Japan; Liancourt Rocks
(Takeshima/Tokdo) disputed with South Korea; Senkaku
Islands (Diaoyu Tai) claimed by China and Taiwan

Sources

This information regarding Japan was retrieved on 12-31
2002 from http://www.odci.gov/cia/publications/factbook/ .

This information is published in the Central Intelligence
Agency's World Factbook. The Factbook is in the public
domain. Accordingly, it may be copied freely without
permission of the Central Intelligence Agency (CIA). The
official seal of the CIA, however, may NOT be copied
without permission as required by the CIA Act of 1949 (50
U.S.C. section 403m). Misuse of the official seal of the CIA
could result in civil and criminal penalties.

Comments and queries are welcome and may be addressed
to:

Central Intelligence Agency
Attn.: Office of Public Affairs
Washington, DC 20505
Telephone: [1] (703) 482-0623
FAX: [1] (703) 482-1739

The World Factbook is prepared by the Central Intelligence
Agency for the use of US Government officials, and the
style, format, coverage, and content are designed to meet
their specific requirements. Information is provided by
Antarctic Information Program (National Science
Foundation), Bureau of the Census (Department of
Commerce), Bureau of Labor Statistics (Department of
Labor), Central Intelligence Agency, Council of Managers of
National Antarctic Programs, Defense Intelligence Agency
(Department of Defense), Department of State, Fish and
Wildlife Service (Department of the Interior), Maritime
Administration (Department of Transportation), National
Imagery and Mapping Agency (Department of Defense),
Naval Facilities Engineering Command (Department of
Defense), Office of Insular Affairs (Department of the
Interior), Office of Naval Intelligence (Department of
Defense), US Board on Geographic Names (Department of
the Interior), US Transportation Command (Department of
Defense), and other public and private sources.

Glossary of Terms

The terms in this glossary are Japanese unless otherwise specified. This glossary contains some terms that are terms that are beyond the scope of this text such as "Kobudo: Old Fighting Art." Kobudo will be the subject of a future edition or an additional guidebook; however, this is a good opportunity to introduce such terms.

A

Age: Rising.
Age tsuki: Rising punch.
Age uke: Rising block.
Ai: "Harmony." This term is most commonly associated with aikido.
Aiki: "Harmony meeting." Combining your energy with your opponent's to gain control.
Ashi: Foot/leg.
Ashi barai: Forward foot sweep.
Ashi kubi: Ankle.
Ashi waza: Foot techniques.
Atemi: Striking.
Atemi waza: Striking techniques.
Awase zuki: Double punch where both fists strike at the same time, one at the head one at the abdomen.

B

Bo: Staff (long).
Bojitsu: Staff techniques (long).
Bugeisha: The formal name for someone who practices bujustsu.
Bunkai: Application of form.
Bushi: Warrior class of Japan.
Bushido: Way of the warrior.
Bujutsu: Fighting arts of the warrior class of Japan.

C

Chi: Chinese name for "spirit," "breath," or "vital energy."
Chishi: Energy stone.
Chikara: Strength or power.
Choku tsuki: Straight punch.
Chudan: Middle (of body, i.e. torso).

D

Dachi: Stance.
Dai Sempai: Most senior student.
Dan: Rank of black belt; 1st dan is the lowest, 10th the highest.
De: Advancing.
Deshi: Disciple or dedicated student.
Do: The Way.
Dojo: Exercise hall, the place where one practices the martial arts.
Doshi: Class member of the same rank.

E

Eku: Oar. Used as a weapon in Okinawan Karate.
Empi: 1. Elbow. 2. Name of a kata (Flying Sparrow)
Empi uchi: Elbow strike. Also Hiji ate.

F

Fumikomi: Stomping kick.

Glossary of Terms

G

Ganmen: Face.
Ganmen shuto: Face knife-hand.
Gedan: Lower, waist or below.
Gedan barai: Low block.
Gedan juji uke: Lower X-block.
Gedan shuto uke: Lower knife-hand block.
Geri: Kick.
Geta: Wooden shoes.
Gi: Uniform for practicing martial arts.
Go: 1. Five 2. Hard
Gohon: Five-finger strike.
Goshi: Hip.
Gyaku: Reverse, reversal.
Gyaku tsuki: Reverse punch (opposite hand and leg).

H

Hachi: Eight.
Hachiji dachi: Open leg stance.
Hachimachi: Headband.
Haishu: Back of the hand.
Haishu uchi: Back hand strike.
Haisoku: Instep.
Haisoku geri: Instep kick.
Haito: Ridge hand (first knuckle of thumb and side of hand).
Haito uchi: Ridge hand strike.
Hajime: Begin.
Hanshi: A respected teacher who is eighth to tenth degree black belt.
Happo: All directional.
Hara: gravity center of the body. Thought to be the source of "ki" or life force. Similar to Tanden.
Hasami zuki: Scissors punch. The opponents front and back are struck simultaneously.
Heisho: Closed.
Heisoku dachi: Closed foot stance.
Hidari: Left (side).

Hiji ate: Elbow strike (upward, downward, forward, rear).
Hiza: Knee.
Hiza geri: Knee strike (upward, side).
Hon: Fingers. See Gohon.
Honbu: Headquarters.

I

Iaido: The Way of the sword.
Ichi (Number) or **Sho** (First): One.
Ippon: One point in a contest.
Ippon ken (tsuki): One knuckle fist.
Ippon kumite: One-step sparring.

J

Jiyu kumite: Free sparring.
Jo: Short staff.
Jodan: Upper, shoulders or above. High.
Jodan juji uke: High X-block.
Jo-Jutsu: Short staff techniques.
Joseke: Upper seat.
Josokutei: Ball of foot.
Ju: 1. Ten 2. Soft
Judo: A martial arts style featuring throwing. Literally, "gentle way." It refers to giving way in order to gain victory.
Judoka: Practitioner of Judo.
Ju-ichi: Eleven.
Juji uke: X-block.
Jutsu: Method.
Jujutsu: The soft method. A grappling art characterized by joint manipulation.

A Goju Ryu Guidebook:
The Kogen Kan Manual for Karate

Glossary of Terms

K

Kagi tsuki: Hook punch.
Kaisho: Open.
Kakato: Heel.
Kamae: Posture.
Kan: House or Hall.
Kano, Jigoro: Founder of Judo.
Kara: Empty.
Karate: Martial arts styles originating in Okinawa. Literally, "empty hand".
Kata: Stylized form, pre-arranged techniques.
Katana: Long sword.
Katsu: Revival techniques.
Kendo: Japanese sword fighting.
Keri waza: Kicking techniques.
Ki: Vital energy.
Kiai: Shout or yell with vital energy (ki).
Kiba dachi: Horse stance.
Kime: Focus.
Kiyotske: Attention.
Kobudo: "Old Fighting Way" This is a method of self defense that uses various weapons adapted from common utensils.
Kohai: Junior class member.
Kokutsu dachi: Back stance.
Koshi: 1. Hip. 2. Ball of the foot.
Koshi waza: Hip techniques.
Ko uke: Bent wrist block.
Ku: Nine.
Kubi: Neck.
Kumite: Sparring.
Kyu: Grade under black belt; 10th kyu is the lowest and 1st the highest.

L

"**L**" is often absent in Japanese words.

M

Ma-ai: Distance.
Mae: Front.
Mae geri: Front kick.
Mae geri keage: Front snap kick.
Mae geri kekomi: Front thrust kick.
Mae tobi geri: Jump front kick.
Makiwara: Punching board.
Mate: Wait. The temporary halt to action.
Mawaru: To turn.
Mawashi geri: Roundhouse kick.
Mawashi tsuki: Roundhouse punch.
Migi: Right (side).
Mikazuki: Crescent.
Mikazuki geri: Crescent kick.
Mikazuki geri uke: Crescent kick block.
Moro: Augmented.
Morote: Two arm or two hand simultaneously.
Morote tsuki: Double forward fist strike.
Morote uke: Double forearm block.
Moro ubi tori: Augmented finger pull.
Mu: Nothing. The state of a clear mind.
Muchimi: Heavy, sticky.
Mushin: Mind of no mind.
Musubi dachi: Attention stance.

N

Nagashi uke: Flowing block.
Nage: Throwing.
Nage waza: Throwing techniques.
Naname: Diagonal.
Neko ashi dachi: Cat stance.
Ni: Two.
Nihon: Double (repetitions).
Nihon nukite: Two finger spear hand. See also Gohon nukite, Nukite.
Ni-ju: Twenty.

Glossary of Terms

Ni-ju-ichi: Twenty-one.
Nukite: Spear hand.
Nunchaku: Flail-like weapon of two rods joined by rope or chain.

O

Obi: Belt.
Oi tsuki: Forward lunge punch (same side hand and leg).
Os: Vernacular for "affirmative," "greeting" and "never give up"
Osae: Pressing.
Otoshi: Downward.

P

Peichin: Okinawan feudal title bestowed on a samurai by a lord.
Pongainoon: The Chinese counterpart of Okinawa's Uechi Ryu Karate.

Q

"Q" is often absent in Japanese words.

R

Randori: Free practice.
Rei: Bow.
Reigisaho: Etiquette.
Roku: Six.
Ryu: Style of school or martial art.
Ryukyu: Okinawa.

S

Sai: Three-pronged metal weapon.
Sakotsu: Collarbone.
San: Three.
Sanchin dachi: Hourglass stance
San-ju: Thirty.

Seika tanden: Lower abdomen
Seiza: Sitting position.
Sempai: Senior class member.
Sensei: Teacher.
Seoi: Shoulder.
Shi: Four.
Shiai: Contest.
Shichi (Number) Nana (seventh): Seven.
Shihan: Master instructor (4th-5th Dan).
Shiho nage: All directions throw.
Shime: Choke.
Shime waza: Choking techniques.
Shimoza: Lower seat.
Shito Ryu: A karate style founded by Kenuwa Mabukni. It is based on Naha Te and Shuri Te.
Shomen: Front.
Shotei: Palm heel.
Shotokan: House of Shoto. A popular Japanese karate style founded by Gichin Funakoshi based on the Okinawan karate Shuri-te. His penname was "Shoto"
Shugyo: Hard practice.
Shuto: Knife-edge hand (little-finger side of palm).
Shuto uchi: Knife hand strike.
Shuto uke: Knife hand block.
Soto: Outside
Sukui nage: Scooping throw.

T

Tameshiwari: Breaking demonstration.
Tanden: Point just below the navel.
Tanto: Short sword.
Tatami: Straw mat.
Tate tsuki: Vertical punch.
Tatte: Command to stand.
Te: Hand. See also Karate.
Tekubi: Wrist.

Glossary of Terms

Tekubi tori: Wrist pull.

Tensho: A kata formulated by Chojun Miyagi Sensei.

Tettsui: Hammer fist; downward strike with closed fist, little finger side as the striking surface.

Te-waza: Hand techniques.

Tonfa: Wooden rod with handle at right angle, used in pairs.

Tori: Attacker; or, pull.

Tsuki: Straight punch; knuckle strike with first two knuckles only. See also Zuki.

Tsuki waza: Punching techniques.

Tsuri: Lifting.

Tuite: 1. Grappling techniques. 2. Using pressure points for joint manipulation.

U

Uchi: Strike. Any direction other than straight.

Uchi Deshi: Special disciple.

Ude: Forearm.

Ude tori: Forearm pull.

Ude uki: Forearm block.

Uke: Block; or, Receiver, to whom techniques are done.

Ukemi: Falling and rolling exercises.

Ukemi waza: Falling techniques.

Ulna: (English) Bone on little-finger side of wrist.

Ulna press: (English) Straight-arm bar with wrist on opponent's elbow.

Ura: Reverse or rear side.

Uraken uchi: Back fist strike.

Ura tsuki: Flip side punch.

Ushiro: Rear or back.

Ushiro geri: Back kick.

V

"V" is often absent in Japanese words.

W

Waza: Technique.

X

"**X**" is common in Chinese words but not Japanese words.

Y

Yama: Mountain.

Yama tsuki: U-punch.

Yame: Stop.

Yari: Spear.

Yoi: Ready.

Yoko: Side.

Yoko geri: Side kick.

Yoko haito: Side ridge-hand.

Yoko kekomi: Side thrust kick.

Yoko otoshi: Side drop.

Yoko shuto: Side knife-hand.

Yoko tobi geri: Jump side kick.

Yubi: Finger.

Yubi tori: Finger pull.

Yudansha: One who is a black belt.

Z

Zanchin: Perfect attention.

Zazen: Sitting meditation.

Zen: 1. Buddhist sect. 2. Religious meditation.

Zenkutso dachi: Front stance.

Zuki: Straight punch. See also Tsuki.

Bibliography

Books

Borkowski, C., & Manzo, M. (1999). *The Complete Idiot's Guide to Martial Arts*. Scarborough, Ontario: Alpha Books.

Bubishi (P. McCarthy Trans.). (1995). Toyko: Charles I. Tuttle Company, Inc.

Cogan, J.P. (2001). *A New Order of Man's History*. Seattle, Washington: Elton-Wolf Publishing. (This is a shameless plug of my father's book. Karate is not mentioned but in its own right it is as high a caliber book as any I have ever read. Thanks Dad!)

Dillman, G. (1992). *Kyusho Jitsu*. Reading, Pennsylvania: George Dillman Karate International

Dillman, G. (1995). *Advanced Pressure Point Grappling*. Reading, Pennsylvania: George Dillman Karate International

Farkas, E., & Corcoran, J. (1983). *The Overlook Martial Arts Dictionary*. Woodstock, New York: The Overlook Press.

Hanzhang, T. (1990). *Sun Tsu's Art of War* (Y. Shibing, Trans.). Brentwood, New York: Sterling Publishing Co., Inc.

Hardy, B. (1992). *Defensive Living*. Pine Bluff, Arkansas: The Defensive Living Press.

Hassell, R.G., & Otis, E. (2000). *The Complete Idiot's Guide to Karate*. Indianapolis: Alpha Books.

Higaonna, M. (1985). *Traditional Karate-Do Okinawa Goju Ryu: Fundamental Techniques* (Vol. 1). Tokyo: Minato Research and Publishing Co., LTD. (out of print).

Higaonna, M. (1986). *Traditional Karate-Do Okinawa Goju Ryu: Performances of the Kata* (Vol. 2). Tokyo: Sugawara Martial Arts Institute Inc. (out of print).

Higaonna, M. (1989). *Traditional Karate-Do Okinawa Goju Ryu: Applications of the Kata* (Vol. 3). Tokyo: Minato Research and Publishing Co., LTD. (out of print).

Bibliography

Higaonna, M. (1990). *Traditional Karate-Do Okinawa Goju Ryu: Applications of the Kata, Part Two* (Vol. 4). Tokyo: Sugawara Martial Arts Institute Inc. (out of print).

Higaonna, M. (1995). *The History of Karate: Goju Ryu.* Westlake Village, California: Dragon Books.

Morgan, F.E. (1992). *Living the Martial Way.* New Jersey: Barricade Books.

Musashi, M. (1982). *A Book of Five Rings* (V. Harris Trans.). Woodstock, New York: The Overlook Press.

Nakayama, M. (1966). *Dynamic Karate* (H. Kauz Trans.). Toyko: Kodansha International.

Oyama, M. (1983) *Mas Oyama's Essential Karate.* New York: Sterling Publishing Company.

Sells, J. (2000) *Unante The Secrets of Karate 2nd Edition* Hollywood: W.H. Hawley Publishing

Toguchi, S. (1976). *Okinawan Goju Ryu.* Burbank, California: O'Hara Publications, Inc.

Webster-Doyle, T. (1988). *Facing the Double-Edged Sword.* Middlebury, Vermont: Atrium Publications.

Video Tapes

Higaonna, M. *Goju Ryu Technical Series* (Vols. 1-5). (1997-1998) [Videotape] Tsunami Videos.

Higaonna, M. *Power Training.* (1994) [Videotape] Tsunami Videos.

Higaonna, M. *Traditional Okinawan Goju Ryu Karate-Do* (Vols.1-24). (1981) [Videotape] San Clemente, California: Panther Productions.

Bibliography

Internet Sites

Analýza pohybù v karate. Retrieved December 12, 2002, from
http://www.fortunecity.com/victorian/bolsover/300/kihon.htm
AWARE Arming Women against Rape and Endangerment. Retrieved December
12, 2002, from
 http://www.aware.org/
Budoseek. Retrieved December 12, 2002, from
http://www.budoseek.net/cgi/hyperseek/hyperseek.cgi
Bushido Online. Retrieved December 12, 2002, from
http://www.bushido-online.com/index1.htm
Castles of Japan. Retrieved December 12, 2002, from
http://www.geocities.com/castlejapan/
Cyber Dojo Forum Retrieved December 12, 2002, from
http://www.cyberdojo.org/
Fighting Arts Magazine. Retrieved December 12, 2002, from
http://www.fightingarts.com/
Goju Ryu Network. Retrieved December 12, 2002, from
 http://gojuryu.net/
Japanese Language. Retrieved December 12, 2002, from
http://japanese.about.com/mlibrary.html
Judo Information Site. Retrieved December 12, 2002, from
http://judoinfo.com/menu.shtml
Karate the Japanese Way: Mark Groenewold. Retrieved December 12, 2002, from
 http://karatethejapaneseway.com/index.html
Martialinfo.com. Retrieved December 12, 2002, from
http://www.martialinfo.com/MartialMainFrame.htm
Martial Spirit. Retrieved December 12, 2002, from
http://www.clubs.psu.edu/JungSimDo/ring.html
Okinawa Kobudo. Retrieved December 12, 2002, from
http://kobudo.okinawa.free.fr/index.html
Okinawa Prefecture's Homepage. Retrieved December 12, 2002, from
http://www.pref.okinawa.jp/index.html
Sabaki Talk Forum. Retrieved December 12, 2002, from
http://users.iafrica.com/a/as/ashihara/webdoc98.htm
Teradex. Retrieved December 12, 2002, from
 http://directory.teradex.com/Sports/Martial_Arts/Karate
Uechi Ryu Karate Do. Retrieved December 12, 2002, from
http://uechi.layer-7.de/perl-bin/createHTML.perl?TXT=stories&LANG=en
Wudan Martial Arts Center. Retrieved December 12, 2002, from
http://www.angelfire.com/art/maa/

<u>*Goju Ryu Special Event Record*</u>

Please note any special seminars, visits to other dojo, gasshuku, and any other special training events.

Date _____ Event _____ Notes _____

Date _____ Event _____ Notes _____

Date _____ Event _____ Notes _____

Date _____ Event _____ Notes _____

Date _____ Event _____ Notes _____

Date _____ Event _____ Notes _____

Date _____ Event _____ Notes _____

Date _____ Event _____ Notes _____

Date _____ Event _____ Notes _____

Date _____ Event _____ Notes _____

Date _____ Event _____ Notes _____

Date _____ Event _____ Notes _____

Date _____ Event _____ Notes _____

Date _____ Event _____ Notes _____

Date _____ Event _____ Notes _____

Date _____ Event _____ Notes _____

Date _____ Event _____ Notes _____

Date _____ Event _____ Notes _____

Date _____ Event _____ Notes _____

Date _____ Event _____ Notes _____

Date _____ Event _____ Notes _____

Date _____ Event _____ Notes _____

Date _____ Event _____ Notes _____

Date _____ Event _____ Notes _____

Goju Ryu Contacts

Friends are important to keep track of. Know the people in your dojo, organization and the martial arts in general. This is a convenient place for some of this information.

Name _____   Name _____
Address _____   Address _____
_____   _____
Phone _____   Phone _____
Email _____   Email _____

Name _____   Name _____
Address _____   Address _____
_____   _____
Phone _____   Phone _____
Email _____   Email _____

Name _____   Name _____
Address _____   Address _____
_____   _____
Phone _____   Phone _____
Email _____   Email _____

Name _____   Name _____
Address _____   Address _____
_____   _____
Phone _____   Phone _____
Email _____   Email _____

Name _____   Name _____
Address _____   Address _____
_____   _____
Phone _____   Phone _____
Email _____   Email _____

Name _____   Name _____
Address _____   Address _____
_____   _____
Phone _____   Phone _____
Email _____   Email _____

A Goju Ryu Guidebook:
The Kogen Kan Manual for Karate

Goju Ryu Contacts

Name _____
Address _____
_____
Phone _____
Email _____

Name _____
Address _____
_____
Phone _____
Email _____

Name _____
Address _____
_____
Phone _____
Email _____

Name _____
Address _____
_____
Phone _____
Email _____

Name _____
Address _____
_____
Phone _____
Email _____

Name _____
Address _____
_____
Phone _____
Email _____

Name _____
Address _____
_____
Phone _____
Email _____

Name _____
Address _____
_____
Phone _____
Email _____

Name _____
Address _____
_____
Phone _____
Email _____

Name _____
Address _____
_____
Phone _____
Email _____

A Goju Ryu Guidebook:
The Kogen Kan Manual for Karate

Goju Ryu Contacts

Name _____
Address _____

_____
Phone _____
Email _____

Name _____
Address _____

_____
Phone _____
Email _____

Name _____
Address _____

_____
Phone _____
Email _____

Name _____
Address _____

_____
Phone _____
Email _____

Name _____
Address _____

_____
Phone _____
Email _____

Name _____
Address _____

_____
Phone _____
Email _____

Name _____
Address _____

_____
Phone _____
Email _____

Name _____
Address _____

_____
Phone _____
Email _____

Name _____
Address _____

_____
Phone _____
Email _____

Name _____
Address _____

_____
Phone _____
Email _____

Name _____
Address _____

_____
Phone _____
Email _____

Name _____
Address _____

_____
Phone _____
Email _____

A Goju Ryu Guidebook:
The Kogen Kan Manual for Karate

A Goju Ryu Guidebook: The Kogen Manual for Karate

Notes

Printed in the United States
By Bookmasters